HOW TO SAY IT
Business Writing That Works

HOW TO SAY IT
Business Writing That Works

The Simple, 10-Step Target Outline System

to Help You Reach Your Bottom Line

ADINA RISHE GEWIRTZ

Prentice Hall Press

PRENTICE HALL PRESS
Published by the Penguin Group
Penguin Group (USA) Inc.
375 Hudson Street, New York, New York 10014, USA
Penguin Group (Canada), 90 Eglinton Avenue East, Suite 700, Toronto, Ontario M4P 2Y3, Canada
(a division of Pearson Penguin Canada Inc.)
Penguin Books Ltd., 80 Strand, London WC2R 0RL, England
Penguin Group Ireland, 25 St. Stephen's Green, Dublin 2, Ireland (a division of Penguin Books Ltd.)
Penguin Group (Australia), 250 Camberwell Road, Camberwell, Victoria 3124, Australia
(a division of Pearson Australia Group Pty. Ltd.)
Penguin Books India Pvt. Ltd., 11 Community Centre, Panchsheel Park, New Delhi—110 017, India
Penguin Group (NZ), 67 Apollo Drive, Rosedale, North Shore 0632, New Zealand
(a division of Pearson New Zealand Ltd.)
Penguin Books (South Africa) (Pty.) Ltd., 24 Sturdee Avenue, Rosebank, Johannesburg 2196,
South Africa

Penguin Books Ltd., Registered Offices: 80 Strand, London WC2R 0RL, England

While the author has made every effort to provide accurate telephone numbers and Internet addresses at the time of publication, neither the publisher nor the author assumes any responsibility for errors, or for changes that occur after publication. Further, the publisher does not have any control over and does not assume any responsibility for author or third-party websites or their content.

First edition: October 2007

Library of Congress Cataloging-in-Publication Data

Gewirtz, Adina Rishe.
　How to say it business writing that works : the simple, 10-step target outline system to help you reach your bottom line / Adina Rishe Gewirtz.—1st ed.
　　p. cm.
　Includes index.
　ISBN 978-0-7352-0425-6
1. Business writing. I. Title.
　HF5718.3.G49 2007
　808'.06665—dc22

808.0606
GEW

　　　　　　　　　　　　　　　　　　　　　　　　　　　　　2007020813

PRINTED IN THE UNITED STATES OF AMERICA

10 9 8 7 6 5 4 3 2 1

Most Prentice Hall Press books are available at special quantity discounts for bulk purchases for sales promotions, premiums, fund-raising, or educational use. Special books, or book excerpts, can also be created to fit specific needs. For details, write: Special Markets, Penguin Group (USA) Inc., 375 Hudson Street, New York, New York 10014.

For Danny
Here, at last, is your book.

ACKNOWLEDGMENTS

Without Jon Franklin, this book would not exist. He taught me to write and think with a clear-eyed logic I was not exactly known for in the poetry of my youth. For that, and for a twenty-year friendship, I thank him and his wonderful wife, Lynn, who brings her own special insight into both writing and life.

Katie McCabe listens with the ear of a great friend and a supreme stylist. I thank her for being the other half of my writing brain, and usually the better one. Many thanks to the amazing Judith Paterson for her guidance and encouragement as this book took shape. Her keen eye and beauty of expression give me much to aspire to.

So many friends read parts of this manuscript or helped with writing samples. Thank you to the fantastic Giliah Litwack, Marla and Charlie Fogelman, Sara Silver, Daniel Friedman, Adam Grumet, and Luke McCabe. And many thanks to Jack McCabe and to Larry Kramer for shepherding me through the contract maze.

A thousand thank-yous to my great agent, Evelyn Fazio, and her partner Pam Brodowsky, who turned my ideas into reality, and to my very smart editor, Jeanette Shaw, who, with her sharp eye and good suggestions, made this a better book.

Books are a family affair at my house, and my extended family on both sides gave me great encouragement. Thanks especially to Adam Rishe, who shared both his business writing and his sense of humor, and to the perpetually energetic Miriam Kramer for her ideas and samples.

Thanks to the dynamic duo—Naomi Schwartz and Rochel Rabinowitz—for the driving/entertaining/child care that allowed this book to be written. And thanks to Josh Rishe and Sima Holland for all the long-distance cheerleading.

My mother, Linda Rishe, is a force of nature when it comes to organization, and that, along with her passion for clear, straight talk, gave me the beginnings of this book. Even more, she's given me the most important of gifts—time. For untold hours of babysitting, errand running, and general rescuing, I can only begin to say thank you.

My father's love, support, and vision made me into a writer. I wish he could have lived to see my name on the cover of a book. But I believe he can still hear my thank you.

Thank you to my built-in research team, Bayla, Shimin, Avital, Gavriella, and Shayna Gewirtz. Their hilarious suggestions, brainstorming, and research help made this book really fun to write.

Finally, and most of all, thank you to my husband, Danny Gewirtz. He insisted (and insisted and insisted) that my method of teaching writing would make a great book. Then he took care of life while I wrote it. This is his book much more than it's mine.

CONTENTS

Part One: The System

Part Two: The System at Work

Part Three: Troubleshooting

Part Four: Exercises

Answer Key

Index

Part One
The System

INTRODUCTION

Writing induces panic.

When Thoreau wrote that most men lead lives of quiet desperation, he was probably inspired by some poor guy in the next cabin, ordered to write a proposal and sweating it. Or maybe he was watching the boss, wading through reams of dense, jumbled writing and trying, against the odds, to keep himself both awake and sane at the same time.

Either way, watching people struggle with writing in the workplace has never been a pretty sight. That's why students often approach business writing as a kind of complex, esoteric art. They memorize numerous templates and forms: for memos, proposals, reports, audits, the friendly business letter, the formal business letter, the marketing letter, the . . . You get the point.

But the truth about business writing is the truth about most writing: there's one process, and if you learn it, the rest will fall into place. Absorb the process, and you can apply it to the world of memos, reports, and audits—even e-mails.

The ten-step process you'll find in this book is called the Target Outline System, which offers you a road map to clear, concise, and, best of all, *organized* business writing. In Part One, you'll learn the system using a simple memo; then, in Part Two, you'll move on to more difficult examples, until you can tackle a complex report and a creative marketing proposal. Part Three offers a series of handy troubleshooting guides to help you check your work, and Part Four lets you practice the system on your own.

Learning a new process takes time, but the Target Outline System is easy to absorb because it's based on how your mind actually works—how readers read and, therefore, how writers ought to write. There are no esoteric rules here—only simple common sense and a technique that helps you craft your message so it's easy on the writer *and* the reader. Learn the ten steps and you'll find that soon your thinking will become more pointed, so that clear writing becomes second nature.

So clear the clutter. Say good-bye to panic and hello to process.

The Target Outline System at a Glance

Step 1: Questions and Research
  1. Who is my audience?
  2. What do they want to know?
  3. What is my bottom line point?
Step 2: Evaluate Your Notes and Determine the Bottom Line
Step 3: Identify the Problem and Resolution
Step 4: Categorize Your Notes
Step 5: Choose Development 3—Point of Insight
Step 6: Choose Development 1—Background
Step 7: Choose Development 2—Bridge
Step 8: Create a List Outline: Organize Categories and Details
Step 9: Add Transitions and an Opening Hook
Step 10: Polish Your Draft

CHAPTER 1

PROBLEMS AND RESOLUTIONS

Everybody likes to talk. We converse by instinct. It's not too hard to transmit information to someone who's standing in front of you. That's because when you talk, your listener is right there, doing half the work. He asks a question, you answer it. He presents a Problem, you respond with your Resolution.

He also keeps you focused. He looks bored when you meander off the point, or dumbfounded when you make a leap in logic he doesn't follow.

When it comes to writing, *poof*, your reader's invisible, and the whole job's on you. Now you've got to figure out what he wants to know: what questions he has and what answers—what Resolution—will satisfy him. Unfortunately, out of sight, the reader's too often out of mind. You forget about keeping his attention. You forget what he wants to know in the first place. You wander off on side trips, get mired in detail, and never get back to the point at all.

To save you from this common writer's malady, you need a road map— clear directions that take into account the reader, what he wants to know, and where you want to take him. This road map keeps your eye on the bull's-eye— the bottom line point that is the reason for the trip in the first place.

To get there on paper, to be a good writer, you must first think about what happens when you read. Stop reading unconsciously and take note of the fact that when you read, you read for a reason. You're looking for something.

For example, why did you pick up this book?

Desperation? Hate business writing but know you need to do it? If that's the case, I'm fairly certain you opened this book curious to see if it could help you out. Your curiosity triggered a desire to seek information—answers—here.

If, on the other hand, you thought *How to Say It* was a guide to better pronunciation, then I'm guessing you'll put the book down any moment now. Your curiosity raised a question, but it was not rewarded with a satisfying answer.

Harness the Reader's Curiosity

When anyone reads or listens to anything, he is looking for some Problem to be resolved. What is all communication really about? I don't know something, and I need or want to know it. That's my Problem. You know it, give it to me, and my Problem is resolved.

Two lessons, then, spring from our little example: first, in order to get a reader's attention, you need to get him to ask a question, so he'll be curious enough to keep reading.

Second, you've got to provide a satisfying answer, or Resolution, to that Problem. This is the underlying structure of all stories—and though business writing is not a once-upon-a-time tale, it shares that structure. Writing in the workplace functions the same way other writing does—it raises an expectation in the reader's mind and carries him along, leading him toward the answer he seeks. It gives it to him piece by piece, until he's satisfied he's gotten the entire thing. Fiction writers call the feeling that keeps the reader reading, looking for answers, suspense. In business writing, which hands the reader information instead of spinning it out in a tale, let's call it basic curiosity.

The underlying structure of any successful piece of writing, then, is the structure that works for stories: get the reader interested by raising a question in his mind, give him the details that unfold the answer, and ultimately resolve the question he's been pursuing all along.

Look at the short story below to see that structure at work:

The Bones of a Story

Two men came upon an old well in the middle of a field.

"How deep do you think it is?" the first one asked.

"Gee, I don't know," his friend answered. "Why don't we drop a rock down there and listen until it hits the bottom? Then we can tell."

They found a stone, threw it in, and listened. It made no sound.

So they found a larger rock and dropped it down. Still nothing. A short distance away they spotted an old railroad tie. It was heavy. Working together, they dragged it across the field, hoisted it up, and heaved it over the edge of the well, letting it drop. At last, they heard a splash.

Suddenly, out of nowhere, a goat came running. It dashed by them and dived right into the well. They were standing scratching their heads, mystified, when a third man came along.

"Have you two by any chance seen a goat?" he asked.

They stared at him, amazed. "Well yes, as a matter of fact," replied the first man. "We just had a goat run past us and jump into this hole!"

"Oh, that couldn't have been my goat," said the third man. "Mine was tied to a railroad tie."

The story above is a joke. Unlike most stories and *all* business writing, jokes rely on the quirk of a surprise ending to get you to laugh. But other than that, a joke shares the elements of good story structure with other types of writing.

For example, what would happen if the story had been written this way?

Two men came upon a well in the middle of a field.

Nearby, a goat was tied to a railroad tie . . .

Groan. With that simple line, I've destroyed the joke. Why? Because I've killed all suspense, and in a joke, that means ruining the punch line.

But what if I began like this, instead?

Did I ever tell you the story about the two guys who drowned a goat with a railroad tie?

Now I've ruined the punch line, but I've maintained the suspense. My joke is transformed into a more traditional little story. Once I've opened this way, I've set up a small Problem for you, the reader. You want to know how it is someone could drown a goat with a railroad tie.

Notice that *I* didn't ask that question, but you did, and you'll wait while I narrate the answer, finishing with the third man's revelation. Question answered. You might not be laughing, but you still sat through the details and waited for the end.

In microcosm, that's how all writing works—even business writing. There are no surprises, joke-like, in expository business writing. But the other elements remain. Business writing, like all writing, relies on a reader's curiosity. It requires that the reader ask a question and it demands that the writer—you—answer that question in a logical, structured way. The only difference between business writing and other forms of writing is the *intent* of that writing. The purpose of a joke is to make you laugh. The purpose of a story is to entertain and inform. Business writing can have any number of purposes: it can persuade, it can sell, it can inform, it can educate. No matter what your topic and what its purpose, however, the "story" must unfold in the way your reader will digest it best.

Story Grammar

The human brain is wired to take in information in a logical format that educators, psychologists, and scientists have been studying for decades. What they've found is that just as very young children learn their native language by fitting the onslaught of words into preexisting patterns in the brain, so we all assimilate information by fitting it—or trying to fit it—into a natural pattern, or "story grammar."

Studies show that when people read a series of information, they both understand and remember it best when it's structured as a story, rather than as a random series. That means that if you put your Resolution in the wrong place, for example, or you fail to set up the situation as a Problem, the reader cannot understand or remember what you've said.

Violating the story structure the brain is primed for is like trying to run software your computer can't read. You'll get an error message. In human beings, this means they'll either stop reading, or, if forced, they'll take the information apart and reorder it into a story they *can* comprehend. Then you'll get these kinds of "error" messages: "What is your point? Why are you telling me things I don't need to know? Where is this going? Who cares?"

Far better to present the information in the *right* order, the writing pattern that matches the reader's thinking pattern, the pattern of Problems and Resolutions. So to begin, let's talk about Problems.

Problems

As my grandmother used to say, everybody has Problems.

And it's a lucky thing, too, because without them, the world would be a pretty dull place. But how do you create a Problem in a piece of writing?

Remember that the Problem raises a question in the reader's mind. In our joke story above, we triggered the question How deep is the well? when we had the first man ask that very question in the second line. But in our anecdotal story, we triggered a different question: "How do you drown a goat with a railroad tie?" simply by asserting the men had done so.

We arrive at the Resolution in both stories when we discover that they mistakenly threw down the railroad tie, unaware the goat was attached. The joke story Resolution comes as a surprise—it doesn't match the question and therefore makes us laugh. But in traditional story structure, we derive satisfaction from getting the answer we sought. Below, see the structure of the second story, which offers just that:

Problem: Railroad tie drowns goat.   *Reader asks: How?*

Men find the well and wonder at its depth.
Men experiment with rocks and don't hear a splash.
Men find and throw down railroad tie, followed by goat.

Resolution: Goat owner explains   *Reader says: Oh, that's how!*
the mystery.

In the tiny story above, the Problem is stated in the very first line. In longer pieces, you'll generally hook the reader with a line or two that leads to the Problem, giving him context and drawing him forward. Nevertheless, the Problem comes very close to the top of your piece of writing, because it's the point of the opening.

Problems in Business Writing

What does a Problem look like in a piece of business writing? It will be the statement, at the very end of your opening, that makes the reader ask that all-important question. Look at the following examples, to see what I mean:

This memo explains why the costs I've incurred could not be avoided.

In our review, we found practices that put Spendthrift Corporation at financial risk.

This proposal sets out our understanding of your needs, an estimate of the fees for our service, and our plan for providing you the highest quality security available.

A new drink, called Brainstorm, offers our company the opportunity to get into the lucrative energy drink market by serving a segment of the market that, while vast, has been all but ignored.

Now why might those be Problems? And to whom?

Again, it all goes back to the reader. In business writing, the Problem is the statement that crystallizes the reader's need. It either reminds him of a need he knows he's got, or causes him to recognize a need he didn't know he had. Either way, it immediately forces him to ask a question, and that question—since it jumped naturally to his mind—will push him to read further, looking for the answer.

Look again at the examples above. How does each crystallize the reader's need?

If the reader is a manager fuming because you're about to blow his budget, he needs to know why you need the money and why he should okay the added expenses. His question is: Why couldn't those costs be avoided?

If the reader is in management at Spendthrift Corporation, the statement that they're at risk creates an urgent need to know more, and find a way out of risk. The reader will ask: What's our risk? How can we minimize it?

If the reader is a client looking for a security system, he'll read the statement from Mercenary Security and ask: What's your plan? What's your price?

And if the reader is the president of a beverage company looking to expand, he'll ask: How will Brainstorm help us grow? What is this unserved market? How will we target it?

With a sharp Problem statement targeted at the right audience, you have cleared the first hurdle of good writing: You've gotten the reader's attention, and you've focused it on a Problem for which you have an answer.

The second point is crucial. If you *don't* have the answer, you'd be a fool to raise the question. Imagine if you opened your memo to the boss on your blown budget, but you really didn't know how it happened. So instead of going on to explain why you exceeded your quarterly funds, you shifted gears and moved on to talk about a wonderful new investment opportunity for the company. How would your reader feel then? Confused. Unsatisfied. Downright irritated. No one likes to ask a question and then see the guy you thought had all the answers wander off on a tangent.

A good Problem statement only works if you've got an equally strong—and matching—Resolution. You've raised a question; you've got to answer it.

The only way to do this is to know where you're headed before you start writing. Your Resolution must be firmly in place *before* you think about presenting a Problem, or you risk a mismatch, at which point your reader, who has plunged into the trip with you, will crash and burn because you jerked him off the road mid-track.

What Is a Resolution?

A Resolution must answer the question raised by the reader. In our little budget memo, this means detailing the expenses that pushed us over, and justifying them. Our opening pushes the reader to ask a question:

We've said: **This memo explains why the costs I've incurred could not be avoided.**

The reader responds: *Great. I'm all ears. Why?*

The only possible Resolution here would be to answer that question.

Problem: Necessity creates expense.

The reader asks: *Why?*

(The body of your memo explains the necessity that caused the expense.)

Resolution: Disaster justifies request.

The reader says: *You're right. After a day like that, you can't avoid spending a little extra.*

Matching the Problem and Resolution is essential. If you don't, you risk telling your reader a joke when he expected an answer. In our railroad tie joke, the bait and switch is what makes it funny—you think the Problem is about how deep the well is, but the point of the story turns out to be a diving goat. Business writing can't rely on bait and switch, or on surprise. It isn't meant to be a joke.

Outside of pure comedy, failure to answer the reader's question means failure, period. No amount of brilliant research or pithy phraseology can save a piece of writing that leaves a reader hanging.

CHAPTER 2

THE TARGET OUTLINE

Problems and Resolutions are the basic building blocks of all writing. The key is to get the reader interested in a question, then give him your answer. If you could picture that graphically, it would look like this:

Keep the image of a target in your mind's eye, because taking the reader from the Problem to the Resolution requires a straight line. You must move toward the *bottom line*—your Resolution—as if you're aiming at a bull's-eye.

It's essential to order your ideas in this way long before you start writing the first complete sentence of your draft. If you wait to decide on your Problem and Resolution in the draft stage, you'll be juggling jobs. You'll be thinking about your reader (if you're smart), and about what you want to say, and about which words to choose, and about what tone is most politic, and about whether that sentence really is a run-on and . . . aagh!

It doesn't take a rocket scientist to figure out that with all those balls in the air, you're going to drop some. And the ones people tend to drop first are the ones called coherence and logic.

The bull's-eye on page 14 saves you from the agony of ripping wandering, messy drafts to shreds after you've wasted several hours and lost a pound in perspiration alone. It's part of the Target Outline, a tool that will help you build a coherent, to-the-point, *effective* piece of writing, no matter what your topic.

The Target Outline helps you see your story in microcosm. It gives you a snapshot of the ideas that make up that story long before you start worrying about wording, sentence structure, and all the other things that come with a draft. It also lets you plan your writing with total focus on how best your reader can accept information—so that your ideas make perfect sense long before you write that first polished sentence.

So relax and take it one step at a time. Master the Target Outline system, and you'll eventually write with greater speed and accuracy, and with a lot less pain.

The Target Outline System

Step 1: Questions and Research

To begin, ask yourself three questions:

1. Who is my audience?
2. What do they want to know?
3. What is my bottom line point?

QUESTION 1: WHO IS MY AUDIENCE?

Audience is always crucial, but it's doubly important in business writing, because in business, your readers are usually the ones paying the bills.

They're also central because without them, information has no meaning.

Imagine, for example, that you were writing a report in which you noted that Coca-Cola had gained market share. What does that mean?

Nothing.

What does it mean if your audience is made up of shareholders in Coca-Cola? Well, then it's good news.

What does it mean if your reader is the chairman of Pepsi-Cola? Not such good news.

Knowing your audience shapes how you will present your information.

Audience also helps determine the context you will need to provide once you start writing. Who are you speaking to? How much do they know?

Technical audiences are those with enough expertise in a topic that they don't need—or want—lengthy definitions of basic terms in the field. If it's 1950 and you're writing to Jonas Salk, who wants to hire you to set up a containment system for his polio research lab, you'd look foolish explaining to him that the disease cripples and kills thousands. On the other hand, since you're selling him a lab containment plan, a detailed explanation of regulations on lab safety would be just right.

On the other hand, when writing for a general audience, don't assume any special expertise. Do, however, assume a basic grade school education. Journalists are taught to write to about an eighth-grade education level. That means when dealing with American readers, you don't explain who George Washington was, but if you're discussing his teeth, you do mention they weren't actually made of wood, but were an uncomfortable combination of human teeth, cow teeth, and ivory, all set in a lead base and attached to a spring.

Once you've given some good thought to who your readers are, give even more to what they want to know.

QUESTION 2: WHAT DO THEY WANT TO KNOW?

This question is almost never hard to answer, if you really think about it. You can't get the reader's attention, or go seek relevant information to answer his questions, without understanding why he's reading in the first place.

In business writing, your reader often tells you what he wants. Clients request proposals for a job or hire you to perform an audit of their books. The boss asks for a how-to manual for the computer software you've developed or calls for ideas for a new marketing push.

In our short memo example, your boss wants to know why you are requesting a budget increase. His question boils down to: Why should I okay this?

What if you're soliciting business on your own, and no one's asked you a question? Or you're writing an essay for broad consumption? Then you've got to marshal your imagination and put yourself in the reader's mind. That's a bit harder, but the trickiest part is remembering to do it. Whether you're trying to sell readers a new widget or teach them a better method to cook an egg, the way into a reader's mind is through his concerns and needs—not your own.

Before you can get the reader to hear your brilliant ideas, you've got to show him you understand those needs. Take a moment to think about them. They'll help shape your writing, help you create a Problem that will get him interested and help you, ultimately, figure out what you're trying to tell him.

That final point brings us to the most important of our three prompts:

QUESTION 3: WHAT IS MY BOTTOM LINE POINT?

Here's where you begin the real work of the writing process. You know who your reader is and what he wants to know—in general. You don't yet know what you want to tell him. His question, so far, is a broad one. Your answer will always be specific.

You can't find that specific answer without doing research, however. You need to gather data so that you can decide, ultimately, what you want to say.

Step 2: Evaluate Your Notes and Determine the Bottom Line

So you get to work. Research can take many forms, but to do efficient research, you can never forget the first two questions—who is my audience, and what do they want to know?

In the short memo justifying your budget request, there will be very little research, per se. Instead, you'll simply make notes for yourself or jot down your "talking points." Let's pretend these are your notes:

Air-conditioning unit fell through the ceiling.

It hit May's chair, and launched her over her desk.

She—and her coffee—landed on me.

Her coffee splashed the computer.

The chair broke.

May left screaming.

I need a new computer, new chair, and new assistant.

I have never exceeded my budget before.

Company's long spent very little on maintenance and facilities. (Which is why the air-conditioning unit came through the ceiling in the first place.)

Pretty bad day at the office. What's the bottom line? That the reader should okay the request because the disastrous air-conditioning cave-in caused all the trouble and explains the need for more money.

Does this answer the reader's question—why should I okay your budget request? It sure does. You have answered Question 3. You've got a bottom line point that addresses your reader's need. It's time to begin writing.

Step 3: Identify the Problem and Resolution

Several years ago I used to teach writing at a large accounting firm. I'd often start my seminars by dragging in a bright bucket, fireman red and with a spiffy handle. After heaving it up onto the desk, where it always made a satisfying *thump*, I'd rummage through it, randomly pulling out bits of paper printed with clever-sounding phrases. Then I'd try to construct a paragraph.

None of the students knew what to make of this. They'd laugh—nervously.

"What are you laughing at?" I'd ask them. "You do this all the time. You just don't have as sharp-looking a bucket."

Most business writers, whether or not they know it, rely on the Bucket School of Writing. They put their focus on words, fishing around for the smartest, most professional phrases they own and throwing them onto the page.

But writing never starts with words. Fine phrases come at the end of the writing process. It starts with ideas.

Step 1 in the process forced you to ask questions and seek answers. Step 2 helped you figure out your bottom line. Steps 3 through 7 take the products of the first two steps and fashion them into a tool you can use: the Target Outline. The Target Outline is nothing like outlines you might have done in high school, where Roman numerals littered the page and you usually created them *after* the draft, because the assignment required it.

Instead, the Target Outline deals in logic. It forces you to pinpoint the central ideas that build to your bottom line point. It's a map—that takes you from your reader's Problem to your Resolution.

The Target Outline

A full Target Outline looks like this:

Problem
Development 1
Development 2
Development 3
Resolution

These five pieces create the structure on which you will hang all your information and ideas, all your recommendations and findings, all your requests and results. The Problem, the Resolution, and the three Developments that get you from one to the other will serve as the major signposts along the journey to your bottom line point. Ultimately, each of the five statements in this outline will balloon into sections of writing. But they stand first as signposts—five distinct points that lead to one bottom line.

How do you use the Target Outline?

Begin at the bottom. Think backwards. The Target Outline has been called an upside-down outline for a number of reasons, the first of which is that you begin where your reader will end.

Go back to Question 3 in Step 1, which had you determine your bottom line point. In our example, we've already culled a "big" answer to our reader's question about why we blew our budget. We've found a bottom line, or Resolution. Here's how it would look in the Target Outline:

Problem:

Development 1:

Development 2:

Development 3:

Resolution: Disaster justifies

expenses.

Wonderful. You've got the answer, now let's put down the question—along with the Problem that prompts it.

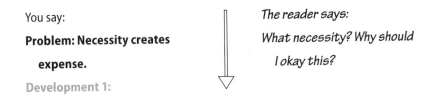

You say:

Problem: Necessity creates

expense.

Development 1:

The reader says:

What necessity? Why should

I okay this?

Development 2:

Development 3:

Resolution: Disaster justifies

expenses.

Oh. That's why!

Notice that our Problem statement—Necessity creates expense—has added a new question to the one the reader's already asked. Since we mentioned that necessity created an unavoidable expense, he's now primed to hear what that necessity might have been. You've responded to his need, but you've done it in a way that directs his focus to *your answer*—the necessity that caused your request for funds.

To continue our snapshot, let's look at the three Developments.

Developments

Why only three Developments? How in the world could three measly Developments hold the information necessary to write a report, or a full-length proposal? Surprise—they can. There are only three Developments in the Target Outline because human beings like their information delivered in a familiar package. They like to be told stories with a beginning, middle, and end. The Target Outline meshes Problem/Resolution and the beginning-middle-end structure of stories—so that when you set up your piece of writing, your reader will absorb what you have to say without working to reorder the pieces of the puzzle.

The Problem and Resolution engage your reader's curiosity, and bring him, willingly, to hear what you've got to say. The Developments then tell him a coherent story.

Each of the three Developments has a role:

Development 1: Background

Development 2: Bridge

Development 3: Point of Insight

DEVELOPMENT 1: BACKGROUND

Development 1 is the place to give the reader essential background, to fill in the context he might still be missing after the bare minimum you used to draw him into your Problem. No matter what kind of piece you're writing—whether you're reporting on a series of events, arguing a point, or even teaching a process—your reader will need some kind of background or context to help him understand the subject at hand.

The information or arguments that follow will rest on this background, and therefore, Development 1, the beginning of your story, will provide it.

Another essential purpose Development 1 can serve is to clear away potential distractions that might detract from your main point. In a persuasive piece, for example, Development 1 would be the place to dispense with opposing arguments. You must show the reader that you have taken into account the other points of view and dismissed them. Otherwise, the reader might argue with you in his head all the way through your writing, distracting him from your subject.

What's the background in our little budget memo? It's both the fact that this is the first time you've been over budget and the fact that the company has long skimped on its facilities budget, which is what caused the assistant-launching, coffee-spilling, computer-breaking accident to begin with.

DEVELOPMENT 2: BRIDGE

Development 2, the Bridge Development, is just that. It connects the background of Development 1 to the crucial last Development, number 3. Although it looks short here, it will usually end up as the longest section in your final piece of writing, because it holds within it most of the information, examples, proofs, and ideas you'll be communicating to your reader. You can think of it as the part of the fairy tale in which Little Red Riding Hood, having met the wolf (Problem) and revealed Grandma's address (Development 1), proceeds to skip through the woods, enter Grandma's house, and put herself in harm's way. But Development 2 ends just where the crucial, climactic action is about to begin. For that, we have the star of the Development show: Development 3.

DEVELOPMENT 3: POINT OF INSIGHT

Development 3 is the place where you present your most compelling proof, example, information, or idea, so that you turn a lightbulb on in the reader's head—what I call a "Point of Insight." Reading that final, crucial idea, proof, or finding, the reader realizes that the only possible Resolution is the one you're about to present.

And that's important, because if the reader can't make that leap of logic on his own, a fraction of a second before you present it to him, he won't buy it. He needs to own the Resolution in the same way he needs to own the Problem: by becoming a participant. Your Problem statement will have prompted him to ask a question—and he'll be the one to articulate and pursue it. Your Development 3 will drive him unfalteringly toward your Resolution—and he'll see it in his own mind before you show it to him on paper. No one likes to be force-fed. Each outline statement helps you prompt the reader and take him along on the journey. But he's got to get into the car willingly. You can't drag him there kicking and screaming.

The Target Outline in Action

Given an understanding of the role of each Development, let's see how the Target Outline might work for our example. We've already determined the Problem and Resolution. Now let's fill in the Developments, too.

Each of the Development statements will ultimately be, like the Problem and Resolution, the bottom line of a whole section of writing. The idea is to pick the crucial overall point of that section and put it down.

Begin with Development 3, because it's the idea most tightly bound to the Resolution. Let's look at Development 3 in the budget memo:

Our Resolution in this case is that the office-breaking disaster that began with a falling air conditioner justifies our request for funds. What will make the reader see that for himself?

Step 4: Categorize Your Notes

To find that answer, it's helpful to go over your notes again, this time labeling them by category. You've got information on the accident, on the damage it caused, on your own history of staying within the budget, and on how the company has spent its money (or not spent it) in the past. By grouping notes into categories, you lift the mass of information into the sphere of ideas:

Air-conditioning unit fell through the ceiling. **ACCIDENT**

It hit May's chair, and launched her over her desk. **ACCIDENT**

She—and her coffee—landed on me. **ACCIDENT**

Her coffee splashed the computer. **DAMAGE**

The chair broke. **DAMAGE**

May left screaming. **DAMAGE**

I need a new computer, new chair, and new assistant. **MY EXPENSES**

I have never exceeded my budget before. **MY BUDGET HISTORY**

Company's long spent very little on maintenance and facilities. (Which is why the air-conditioning unit came through the ceiling in the first place.) **COMPANY'S BUDGET HISTORY**

Now you've got categories to choose from: ACCIDENT, DAMAGE, MY EXPENSES, MY BUDGET HISTORY, and the COMPANY'S BUDGET HISTORY.

Notice there's nothing fancy about how I labeled each piece; almost any general categorizing will do. But now, instead of nine distinct pieces of information, I've got five categories. There's no magic to this particular number. It could as easily be six or twenty. What it gives me is a more manageable way to see my facts. Now they're not simply details. They're also pieces of larger ideas.

Step 5: Choose Development 3—Point of Insight

ACCIDENT

DAMAGE

MY EXPENSES

MY BUDGET HISTORY

COMPANY'S BUDGET HISTORY

Which of the categories seems most likely to convince our reader that I am justified in asking for more money? It's got to be the *expenses* caused by the damage my computer (and everything else) sustained. Although the accident is pretty spectacular, it would be irrelevant if it hadn't ended with a broken computer and a crazed assistant. Therefore, label the category EXPENSES as Development 3.

Why? Because once the reader sees what you need to spend the money on, he realizes that your expenses are justified.

Therefore, the bottom line of our Development 3, the Point of Insight, will be something like: Damage creates need.

Now the outline will look like this:

You say:

Problem: Necessity creates

   expense.

Development 1:

Development 2:

The reader says:

What necessity? Why?

**Development 3: Damage creates
 need.**
Resolution: Disaster justifies
 expenses.

Oh boy, I can see that.

Oh, that's why! Okay. I agree.

A NOTE ABOUT OUTLINE STATEMENTS

Looked at alone, outline statements can often sound a lot like platitudes: "Damage creates need," for example. Remember, however, that these statements are the culmination of information—proof—that you're going to deliver to the reader. That information will make him *see* your point, so the outline statement will no longer sound like an unfulfilled promise. Keep in mind that the statements are signposts for you, the writer. Never write a statement you can't make real with information. Facts are the fuel that makes the outline work.

Step 6: Choose Development 1—Background

Development 3 might be the star of the Development show, but it can't stand on its own. Focus next on Development 1: What background must the reader understand in order to launch him into this topic?

First, let's see what background we have. What is the crucial context our reader will need to understand and—equally important—accept our request? That will be the information that we've never blown our budget before and, also, the little bit of history about the company skimping on maintenance and repair, which triggered that interesting Monday in the office.

So what goes into our background section? The categories MY BUDGET HISTORY and the COMPANY'S BUDGET HISTORY. What bottom line do these boil down to? The idea that, despite the fact that the company has skimped, the writer can be trusted. He's never asked for more money before. Our outline would now look this way:

You say:	The reader says:
Problem: Necessity creates expense.	*What necessity? Why?*
Development 1: We remain trustworthy.	*That's true, and I'll give you a fair hearing because of it.*
Development 2:	
Development 3: Damage creates need.	*Oh boy, I can see that!*
Resolution: Disaster justifies expenses.	*It sure does!*

Step 7: Choose Development 2—Bridge

Finally, what does the reader still need to know? The answer to that question should be the idea you place in Development 2. This bridge must serve to connect Development 1 to Development 3. Ask yourself: What piece of logic is missing?

In this case, the answer is obvious. He needs to see what caused all that damage. That would be a combination of the categories labeled ACCIDENT and DAMAGE. The bottom line of those two categories put together? Something simple, like Accident, causes damage.

You say:	The reader says:
Problem: Necessity creates expense.	*What necessity? Why?*
Development 1: We remain trustworthy.	*That's true, and I'll give you a fair hearing because of it.*
Development 2: Accident causes damage.	*It most certainly does!*

Development 3: Damage creates
need.

Resolution: Disaster justifies
expenses.

Oh boy, I can see that!

It sure does!

Voilà! The logic of your argument is firmly in place. You've drawn the reader in by tapping into a need he has: to understand why you want more money. You earned his trust by showing him you've been trustworthy in the past, detailed the accident that caused the damage, and made a list of the expenses for which you're requesting the funds. Finally, you'll ask for a specific action on his part—signing off on the expenses—once he sees that they are justified.

Wonderful! Without writing a single polished sentence or reaching once into your "phrase bucket," you've given your piece a solid shape.

Instead of wandering through the woods, getting lost in the thicket of facts and figures, you've taken an aerial view of your piece, seen a snapshot of your ideas and how you'll lay them out at a glance. But the devil is in the details, as any struggling writer—in other words, *every* writer—knows. Wonderful as the Target Outline is, it does not deal in detail. So it's time to meet the second half of the system—which does.

CHAPTER 3

THE LIST OUTLINE

Earlier I called the Target Outline an upside-down outline. That's true not only because you begin your thinking where your reader will end his. It's also true because of the structure of the outline itself. Each of the outline statements in the Target Outline in the last chapter are not headlines, as in other outlining systems. You don't sit them on top of the page and then elaborate underneath.

Instead, as I've said, they're *bottom lines.* Each is the point you're driving toward in your writing of that "chunk" of the piece. A chunk can be almost any length, from a paragraph to a chapter or more. What's crucial is that it must contain all the ideas, facts, and examples that make the point of that outline statement. If you're writing the chunk heading toward Development 1—where you remind the reader of your budget history, and that of the company's—then that chunk will include the facts that you've always stayed within budget before and that the company has historically skimped on maintenance.

Though we have few facts to juggle in our budget memo, think how complicated it might be if your background section had many more pieces of information and included numerous ideas. The Target Outline helps you create the big picture, but the List Outline guides your organization down to the sentence level. It organizes the details so they'll work to make each point you need to move down the road, taking you, incrementally, toward that final destination, the Resolution.

To create a List Outline, space out your Target Outline statements, leaving room *above* each one. You'll want to organize your details so they drive toward each bottom line. A List Outline will look like this:

Here you get the reader's attention and prompt him to ask that all-important question . . .

Problem: Your Problem Statement Here

Then add facts and figures and other information to give the reader essential background . . .

Development 1: Your Background Statement Here

So that he can begin to understand the information and ideas you're showing him, carefully building your logic so that . . .

Development 2: Your Bridge Statement Here

You can show him the one crucial piece that will make him see the bottom line that's coming . . .

Development 3: The Point of Insight Here

And realize that your data is convincing, and your logic is flawless.

Resolution: Your Resolution Statement Here

Step 8: Create a List Outline—Organize Categories and Details

To apply this to our budget memo, first simply insert your note categories in the right place in your List Outline. It helps also to keep a copy of the original Target Outline handy, so you know where you're going as you fill in more details and sometimes take more than one page. Having done that, your new List Outline will look this way:

Original Target Outline

Problem: Necessity creates expense.

Development 1 (Background): We remain trustworthy.

Development 2 (Bridge): Accident causes damage.

Development 3 (Point of Insight): Damage creates need.

Resolution: Disaster justifies expenses.

List Outline:

Problem: Necessity creates expense.

COMPANY'S BUDGET HISTORY
MY BUDGET HISTORY

Development 1 (Background): We remain trustworthy.

ACCIDENT
DAMAGE

Development 2 (Bridge): Accident causes damage.

MY EXPENSES

⬇

Development 3 (Point of Insight) Damage creates need.

⬇

Resolution: Disaster justifies expenses.

Notice first that you've got two empty chunks—Problem and Resolution. What goes there? Think back to your questions. For the Problem, look to Questions 1 and 2. Who is my reader and what does he want to know? The Problem chunk is where you prompt the reader to ask his question. In this case, you want the reader asking: Why should I okay your budget request?

What will make him ask that? Simply stating, as we mentioned above, that necessity created the expense—it was unavoidable.

For the Resolution, we have the answer to Question 3—our bottom line. This is the fact that the disaster justifies our expense request, so he should okay it. Simply add that point into the chunk above the Resolution.

This is not the time to worry about exact words. We're interested here in the details, but still on a high level—we want to know how we'll organize them, not what they'll eventually sound like. So, in a general way, fill the Problem and Resolution chunks before you go on:

This memo explains why the costs I've incurred could not be avoided.

⬇

Problem: Necessity creates expense.

MY BUDGET HISTORY
COMPANY'S BUDGET HISTORY

⬇

Development 1 (Background): We remain trustworthy.

```
┌─────────────────────────────────────────────────────┐
│                      ACCIDENT                        │
│                       DAMAGE                         │
└─────────────────────────────────────────────────────┘
                          ▼▼

**Development 2 (Bridge): Accident causes damage.**


┌─────────────────────────────────────────────────────┐
│                     MY EXPENSES                      │
└─────────────────────────────────────────────────────┘
                          ▼▼

**Development 3 (Point of Insight): Damage creates need.**


┌─────────────────────────────────────────────────────┐
│  Please sign off on these additional expenses.       │
└─────────────────────────────────────────────────────┘
                          ▼▼

**Resolution: Disaster justifies expenses.**
```

Next, look at the chunks that have more than one category of notes: Developments 1 and 2. We don't have much to order here, but we still must decide which piece of information comes first and which last. Always write to your bottom line, because that is the point you want to have stay with your reader. The rest builds to that. In Development 1, for example, the point is that we're trustworthy, because we've never before exceeded our budget. This is despite the fact that the company scrimps on maintenance. Therefore, the company's history goes first and leads to the information about us.

In Development 2, we've got both the damage the accident caused and the accident itself. Logically, the reader needs to know about the accident before he can understand how the damage happened. Organization within the outline chunk is the same as organization on the Target Outline level. Background or context comes first. The most important point comes near the bottom, and the other facts should *make* that point.

Order it that way.

Once you've gotten your categories in order, it's time to return to the actual notes, so we can organize on an even finer level of detail. The List Outline, with notes filled in, now looks this way:

This memo explains why the costs I've incurred could not be avoided.

Problem: Necessity creates expense.

The company has long spent very little on maintenance and facilities.
I have never exceeded my budget before.

Development 1 (Background): We remain trustworthy.

Air-conditioning unit fell through the ceiling.
It hit May's chair, and launched her over her desk.
She—and her coffee—landed on me.
Her coffee splashed the computer.
The chair broke.
May left screaming.

Development 2 (Bridge): Accident causes damage.

I need a new computer, chair, and assistant.

Development 3 (Point of Insight): Damage creates need.

Please sign off on these additional expenses.

Resolution: Disaster justifies expenses.

Our draft is taking shape even before we've begun drafting. There are only two more features of the List Outline that will move it from outline to draft: transitions and the opening hook.

Step 9: Add Transitions and an Opening Hook

TRANSITIONS

Transitions connect ideas both between parts of the outline—when one chunk ends and another begins—and within a chunk, where they connect the details. Their essential role is to keep the reader on track, so that he can follow as you move from topic to topic or idea to idea. Transitions can be as simple as a skipped line to signal a shift in subject, or a phrase like "We also found . . ."

Transitions can also be complex, a subject we'll discuss as we deal with more complicated pieces in later chapters. In our budget memo, they'll be simple.

Where do we need transitions in the budget memo?

Look first to the beginning of each chunk. In the opening of the Background chunk, we simply jump into the information that the company has spent very little on maintenance in the past. It would be nice to draw the reader into that, instead of making it sound like a flat accusation. To show him that this will be relevant, a simple transition like "As you know, we have been on a tight budget for some time . . ." would smooth the way into the history.

In the opening of the Bridge section, we currently just list what happened, starting with "Air-conditioning unit fell . . ." These are notes. We ended the chunk above with the statement that we've never exceeded our budget before. Now we need to orient the reader—turn him back in time—to the events of the accident. For this we could use a simple "Unfortunately [which sets the tone], last Monday [which sets the time] the air-conditioning unit . . ."

Finally, we need a transition from the events of the accident to the Point of Insight chunk—the list of our expenses. Again, we need to give the reader a bridge. How about this? "The accident [which refers back to what we just described] resulted in the following unavoidable expenses:"

With these additions, our List Outline will look this way:

This memo explains why the costs I've incurred could not be avoided.

Problem: Necessity creates expense.

Transition: As you know, we have been on a tight budget for some time . . .

The company has long spent very little on maintenance and facilities.

I have never exceeded my budget before.

Development 1 (Background): We remain trustworthy.

Transition: Unfortunately, last Monday . . .

Air-conditioning unit fell through the ceiling.

It hit May's chair, and launched her over her desk.

She—and her coffee—landed on me.

Her coffee splashed the computer.

The chair broke.

Development 2 (Bridge): Accident causes damage.

Transition: The accident resulted in the following unavoidable expenses:

new computer, chair, and assistant.

Development 3 (Point of Insight): Damage creates need.

Please sign off on these additional expenses.

Resolution: Disaster justifies expenses.

THE OPENING HOOK

The opening hook is a kind of transition, too. It takes the reader from what's out there—in life—to the world of your piece of writing. The opening hook must both draw his attention and immediately orient him to your subject. Forget the opening hook, and your reader will feel like he's walked in halfway through someone else's conversation. He'll be disoriented, and he'll either leave or miss the opening facts while he tries to orient himself.

Opening hooks can get really fancy—another topic we'll discuss later—but in our budget memo, and in much of business writing, the opening hook is as simple as a subject line or a salutation. Put the subject front and center and you've opened the car door for your reader. Now he can settle in and embark on the journey to your point.

In this case, since we're writing an informal memo, frame it as a letter or e-mail. That means the opening hook addresses the reader by name. It then moves on to its orienting role—to give the reader needed context. Here that means immediately stating the subject of the memo and acknowledging the Problem it addresses—that our request has caused our department to exceed its budget.

The opening hook of our budget memo, then, will read this way: "Dear Jim, You asked me to justify my request for a budget increase this quarter. I realize this increase will cause our department to significantly exceed its facilities and administration budget. However . . ."

Put that in and the outline is done. Here it is:

> Dear Jim,
> You asked me to justify my request for a budget increase this quarter. I realize this increase will cause our department to significantly exceed its facilities and administration budget. However, this memo explains why the costs I've incurred could not be avoided.

Problem: Necessity creates expense.

Transition: As you know, we have been on a tight budget for some time . . .

The company has long spent very little on maintenance and facilities.

I have never exceeded my budget before.

Development 1 (Background): We remain trustworthy.

Transition: Unfortunately, last Monday . . .

Air-conditioning unit fell through the ceiling.

It hit May's chair, and launched her over her desk.

She—and her coffee—landed on me.

Her coffee splashed the computer.

The chair broke.

Development 2 (Bridge): Accident causes damage.

Transition: The accident resulted in the following unavoidable expenses:
new computer, chair, and assistant.

Development 3 (Point of Insight): Damage creates need.

Please sign off on these additional expenses.

Resolution: Disaster justifies expenses.

Evaluating the List Outline

Before moving on, evaluate your outline. Ask yourself:

1. Does the logic hold together? Does each point lead smoothly to the next?
2. Do all the points drive toward the bottom line of that chunk?
3. Is anything missing?

In longer pieces, when you lay out your data in the List Outline, you'll often notice pieces missing. Once you lay the logic out graphically, it's easier to spot gaps. When that happens, it's time to return for more research. In that case, though, your research will be directed. You'll no longer cast the net wide, but zero in on just what was missing and go find it. To find more on directed research, see Chapter 9, page 147. For now, however, writing a short memo without gaps, we're ready to move on to the draft.

CHAPTER 4

THE DRAFT

Once the ideas line up, the logic works, the transitions connect, and the outline rushes forward to the bottom line point, only one task remains: Don't sabotage yourself in the draft stage. In the world of work, people often mistake big words for big thoughts. They're wrong. Your main job in polishing the draft will be to rein in the urge to speak anything but everyday English.

Step 10: Polish Your Draft

Begin polishing your draft by re-reading your List Outline, filling in full sentences where notes or phrases remain, and correcting the obvious: typos, misspellings, errors in grammar, or random shifts in tense, from past to present or vice versa. Make sure subjects agree with predicates; make sure you don't start a sentence with "she" and switch to "they" halfway through. Check yourself when the computer alerts you to a mistake. Find out what's wrong with your sentence and rewrite it.

Once you've corrected the obvious, you can spend some time figuring out exactly how you want to express your thoughts. Each writer has a unique style. That's fine. Just make sure yours isn't called "impenetrable." To improve your style, consider the following suggestions:

WORDS

Use enough variation so the reader doesn't feel like he's heard the same phrase or term over and over. But don't try to improve on invisible verbs like "said" or "wrote" with fancier ones like "stated" or "declared." You want the reader to pay attention to your ideas, not your stilted phraseology.

Business writing, more than any other type, should be clear. Your reader shouldn't really "see" your language—he should be hearing your ideas. Don't throw up an opaque screen of odd-sounding terms. Let your message speak for itself.

To that end, use simple, everyday words as much as possible. Use active verbs that speed sentences along, and avoid turning verbs into nouns: analyze something, don't "do an analysis"; investigate, don't "conduct an investigation." The reader wants to get where you're taking him—to the point—without being slowed by roadblocks like muddy language and twisted phrases.

Most of all, if that annoying blowhard, Jargon, seems to want to join the trip, run as fast as you can the other way.

JARGON

In the unlikely event that you haven't gotten to know him, Jargon is that miserable know-it-all everybody hates to have at a party. He's pompous, verbose, and impenetrable. Most people understand only about half of what he's saying at any given time. If a normal, ordinary word will work, Jargon despises it. He reaches for the acronym or technical phrase every time.

Jargon abuses words. He turns perfectly healthy verbs into sickly, ugly-sounding phrases filled with nouns. If he means you should "study," he'll say "a study is to be performed"; if he wants you to search, he'll tell you to "ascertain that a search is conducted." Or he'll do the opposite, taking simple, unobtrusive nouns like "incentive" and transforming them into monstrous, unnatural verbs, like "incentivize."

The interesting thing about jargon is that it's so changeable. A word is jargon depending on who's listening, and that's where awareness of your reader surges again to the fore. If a group of electrical engineers gathers to talk, we wouldn't expect them to avoid using words like "amplitude" and "attenuation." They all understand those words and use them as part of their work.

But ask an electrical engineer to write something for the rest of us, and words like "amplitude" sound like Greek. So the first rule of jargon is: Know to whom you speak. You might understand and love a word, but if it's going to sound like a foreign tongue to your reader, it's jargon.

ACRONYMS

The same rule applies to acronyms, but more so. Writers commonly employ acronyms to avoid repeating long phrases too often. But cram too many acronyms into a small space and your paragraph turns into alphabet soup. Even an expert reader will have a hard time keeping track of which acronym is which if you've got more than three of them in a sentence or short paragraph. Again, keep your eye on the reader. Spell out all acronyms on the first reference, then try not to use more than three in one cramped space.

PASSIVE CONSTRUCTIONS

Active verbs show someone doing something. Passive verbs create victims who are acted *upon*. Bureaucratic writers litter their prose with passive constructions, mostly to avoid assigning anyone responsibility for anything. The mistaken report *was* submitted, so we don't have to find out that Albert in Personnel made the mistake. Sentences move better when the subject of the sentence acts through its verb.

Don't dump the entire roster of "to be" verbs in the garbage, however. Use them when you want to describe a state of being or a rule: "Carol is smart" works much better than the preposterous "Intelligence defines Carol" or the over-the-top "Carol sparkles with smarts."

POMPOSITY AND FAKERY

Finally, *always* avoid the pompous words that are jargon no matter who's reading. To see what that means, look at the snippet below, from an audit by a large accounting firm:

"The acquisition was accounted for using the purchase method of accounting. The company preliminarily allocated approximately $—— to intangible assets and approximately $—— to goodwill which are being amortized over a seven year period for book purposes . . . There has been no recordation of purchased Research and Development. The appropriateness of this treatment is assessed below."

Don't fall into the bad habit of taking perfectly fine English words like "first" and turning them into blowhards like "preliminarily." As for "the appropriateness of this treatment is assessed below," what's wrong with: "We assess this treatment below"? Finally, please don't make up words like "recordation." That's just plain nasty.

SENTENCES

Some writers will tell you to stick to short sentences no matter what. I disagree. Stick too many short sentences together, and you've got us reading *The Cat in the Hat.* I loved that book, but it's not exactly Shakespeare. Sentence length should vary depending on what you're trying to say.

Long sentences, and the occasional passive construction that comes with them, slow the pace of a piece of writing. This is not all bad. At the beginning of a piece, or when explaining complex material, you might want to slow down a little to give the reader a chance to breathe—and absorb your ideas.

Short sentences rev the engine. Use them when you're getting close to your point. A mix of long and short sentences—used appropriately—creates rhythm. Listen to your writing with your ear. Read it aloud. Think like the reader. Do that, and rhythm will come.

TONE

Tone is the way in which you address your reader. Are you informal, using colloquialisms and making the occasional personal reference? Or are you formal, holding the reader at arm's length and exuding professionalism?

As with everything else in writing, decide on tone by knowing your audience. In our budget memo, you can probably refer to your manager by his first name, but you're obviously not too close. Remember, he's so out of the loop he doesn't know about your air-conditioning fiasco. Therefore, talking about your former assistant as "May" and describing how she ran screaming from the room would be too informal for him. Instead, step back. Polish up your language and delete personal asides.

FORMATTING

Make your writing easy on the eye as well as the ear. Leave plenty of white space around your paragraphs. Break overly long paragraphs in two. And when dealing with complex data, make liberal use of headings, bullets, and lists—anything that can help your reader absorb what you're offering.

Look at the difference in the following two examples, to see what I mean:

Before

The accident resulted in the following unavoidable expenses: a new computer, a new desk chair, and a new assistant.

After

The accident resulted in the following unavoidable expenses:

1. New personal computer
2. New desk chair
3. New administrative help

Which is easier on the eye? Use white space and give your facts some breathing room. Don't worry about wasting paper; we all recycle.

The Full Draft

Give yourself a pat on the back. You're done. You've plotted your ideas, organized the details so they move in a straight line to each of your main points, turned notes into full sentences, eliminated mistakes and jargon, polished your sentences to a high sheen, and formatted for ease of reading. Take a look at the final draft, with the List Outline elements included in bold and parentheses and the Target Outline in capital letters. You'd pull those out of the real final product. Notice, too, that the guideposts—those Target Outline statements—are not literally in the draft. They simply directed you to make the right point.

(opening hook)

Dear Jim,

You asked me to justify my request for a budget increase this quarter. I realize this increase will cause our department to significantly exceed its facilities and administration budget. However, this memo explains why the costs I've incurred could not be avoided.

PROBLEM: NECESSITY CREATES EXPENSE.

(transition) As you know, we have been on a tight budget for some time, and the company has chosen not to invest a great deal of money in maintenance and repair of our current facility. Despite this, we have never before exceeded our quarterly budget or requested an increase.

D1: WE REMAIN TRUSTWORTHY.

(transition) Unfortunately, last Monday the air-conditioning unit fell through that hole that's been slowly spreading in the office roof. It landed on the back of my assistant's swivel chair. As she was sitting in it at the time, drinking coffee, the impact launched her over her desk. She landed in my cubicle, spilling coffee on my keyboard and screen, and shorting out the computer.

D2: ACCIDENT CAUSES DAMAGE.

(transition) The accident resulted in the following unavoidable expenses:

1. New personal computer

2. New desk chair

3. New administrative help

D3: DAMAGE CREATES NEED.

If you could sign off on these additional expenses, I'd appreciate it.

R: DISASTER JUSTIFIES EXPENSES.

Part Two
The System
at Work

In the next few chapters, we'll review the system as it applies to different types of business writing. Although the Target Outline System is no different whether you're writing a memo or a proposal, a report or an evaluation, it helps to see it play out in different ways, depending on the assignment.

Each chapter that follows will show you a writing category, pinpoint the intent of that category, then choose an example and apply the system. The examples I've chosen are based on fictional situations, even if they are drawn from history. Take any "facts" with a grain of salt and focus on the writing process and the structure of each piece as it evolves.

CHAPTER 5

LETTERS AND E-MAILS

Letters and e-mails form the backbone of business communication. Once you master the Target Outline System, you'll often be able to skip some of the later steps in the process because they'll come so naturally. When writing a short letter, for example, you can probably rely on the Target Outline to organize you, without doing a formal List Outline. Here, however, we'll go through the entire process, so that when you need it, you'll know how to do it.

Intent: Letters and e-mails can communicate almost anything:

- Thanks
- Commendation
- Confirmation of receipt
- Summary of an agreement or discussion
- Complaints
- Regrets

Bottom Line: The bottom line of most letters and e-mails is to:

- Convey information
- Get the reader to take an action

The System in 10 Easy Steps

You are the principal of a small private school where one Thomas Alva Edison is a student. His teachers complain about him daily. He daydreams. They call him "addled," and, altogether, you doubt he has a very bright future (pardon the pun). You've got the rotten job of communicating this to his mother, who will most certainly *not* take the news well. How do you write the letter?

Step 1: Questions and Research

1. **Who is my audience?** Mrs. Nancy Edison
2. **What does she want to know?** How is her boy Tom doing in school?
3. **What is my bottom line point?** (see Step 2)

Find out:

- What teachers say about Thomas
- Thomas's weaknesses
- Thomas's strengths
- What previous contact, if any, there has been with Mrs. Edison
- What action the school wants Mrs. Edison to take
- What action the school plans/hopes to take

Step 2: Evaluate Your Notes and Determine the Bottom Line

Here are your notes:

Thomas's teacher called him addled.
Thomas spends most of his time daydreaming.

When asked what he was thinking about, Thomas said he was "imagining things."

Thomas doesn't know his history.

Thomas does a little better in math and science, but only when he's paying attention.

Thomas spent one morning fiddling with the school's gas lamp rather than practicing his penmanship, which is very poor.

Thomas's teacher reports that when called on to recite, he does not know the material. Neither can he name the states of the Union. His spelling is atrocious.

The bottom line? Thomas needs to shape up or he will surely fail.

Step 3: Identify the Problem and Resolution

You say:

Problem: Thomas has been having trouble in school.

Resolution: Thomas needs to shape up or he will surely fail.

The reader says:

What kind of trouble?

I'd better get that boy some help!

Step 4: Categorize Your Notes

Thomas's teacher called him addled. **THOMAS'S DAYDREAMING**

Thomas spends most of his time daydreaming. **THOMAS'S DAYDREAMING**

When asked what he was thinking about, Thomas said he was "imagining things." **THOMAS'S DAYDREAMING**

Thomas doesn't know his history. **THOMAS'S POOR PERFORMANCE**

Thomas does a little better in math and science, but only when he's paying attention. **THOMAS'S STRENGTHS**

Thomas spent one morning fiddling with the school's gas lamp rather than practicing his penmanship, which is very poor. **THOMAS'S DAYDREAMING, THOMAS'S POOR PERFORMANCE**

Thomas's teacher reports that when called on to recite, he does not know the material. Neither can he name the states of the Union. His spelling is atrocious. **THOMAS'S POOR PERFORMANCE**

Step 5: Choose Development 3—Point of Insight

Here are your categories:

THOMAS'S DAYDREAMING

THOMAS'S POOR PERFORMANCE

THOMAS'S STRENGTHS

If the bottom line is that Thomas must shape up or he'll surely fail, which point will most show that the child is on the verge of failure? It's got to be Thomas's poor performance. Label that D3 and put it into your outline:

You say:

Problem: Thomas has been
   having trouble in school.

Development 1 (Background):

Development 2 (Bridge):

**Development 3 (Point of
   Insight): Thomas performs
   poorly.**

Resolution: Thomas needs to
   shape up or he will surely fail.

The reader says:

What kind of trouble?

*Oh no—poor spelling? However
   will he succeed in life?*

I'd better get that boy some help!

Step 6: Choose Development 1—Background

Next, what background does Mrs. Edison need? Although you could choose to put in the history of Thomas's daydreaming, that's really more to the point of the letter. When writing an argument—trying to prove a point—it's best to put opposing points of view first. This is also true when writing criticism. Put any praise front and center, both to soften the blow and to show you acknowledge the other side.

Therefore, Thomas Edison's facility with math ought to be Development 1. Label it and fill in your outline:

You say:	The reader says:
Problem: Thomas has been having trouble in school.	*What kind of trouble?*
Development 1 (Background): Thomas can do well.	*Of course! My boy's a genius!*
Development 2 (Bridge):	
Development 3 (Point of Insight): Thomas performs poorly.	*Oh no—poor spelling? However will he succeed in life?*
Resolution: Thomas needs to shape up or he will surely fail.	*I'd better get that boy some help!*

Step 7: Choose Development 2—Bridge

What's left? The daydreaming, which makes up the middle of the letter. That's what's causing Edison to forget his history and be a poor speller. Label it, and fill in your complete Target Outline:

You say:		The reader says:
Problem: Thomas has been having trouble in school.		*What kind of trouble?*
Development 1 (Background): Thomas can do well.		*Of course! My boy's a genius!*
Development 2 (Bridge): Thomas daydreams.		*In school, too?*
Development 3 (Point of Insight): Thomas performs poorly.		*Oh no—poor spelling? However will he succeed in life?*
Resolution: Thomas needs to shape up or he will surely fail.		*I'd better get that boy some help!*

Step 8: Create a List Outline—Organize Categories and Details

Problem: Thomas has been having trouble in school.

Development 1: Thomas can do well.

Development 2: Thomas daydreams.

Development 3: Thomas performs poorly.

Resolution: Thomas needs to shape up or he will surely fail.

Problem: Thomas has been having trouble in school.

Thomas does a little better in math and science.

Development 1: Thomas can do well.

Thomas's teacher called him addled.

Thomas spends most of his time daydreaming.

When asked what he was thinking about, Thomas said he was "imagining things."

Development 2: Thomas daydreams.

Thomas spent one morning fiddling with the school's gas lamp rather than practicing his penmanship, which is very poor.

Thomas doesn't know his history.

Thomas's teacher reports that when called on to recite, he does not know the material. Neither can he name the states of the Union. His spelling is atrocious.

Development 3: Thomas performs poorly.

Resolution: Thomas needs to shape up or he will surely fail.

Notes: In a short letter like this one, there's not much to organize within chunks. In Development 3, however, notice that we gain effectiveness if we move from Thomas's daydreaming (fiddling with the gas lamps) to the results of his daydreaming—weakness in history, recitation, and spelling. In this way, the first note in the section, which was originally labeled both DAYDREAM-ING and POOR PERFORMANCE, functions as a transition between the two. Double-labeled notes can often work as bridges between sections.

The empty Problem chunk will be filled with the opening hook and an explanation of why you're writing, which should include a statement of the Problem; the empty Resolution chunk will be filled with the Resolution statement and with closing remarks—encouraging Mrs. Edison to be in touch, for example, with any questions.

Step 9: Add Transitions and an Opening Hook

Transitions are almost unnecessary here, as the material is so closely connected. However, after complaining about Thomas's "imagining things," you might want to note that you do value imagination, just not at the expense of, say, spelling. This would further connect Thomas's daydreaming to his poor performance.

The opening hook will be the opening of the letter—a salutation.

Step 10: Polish Your Draft

In any letter, but especially in one that voices criticism, make sure you have made no mistakes. Don't complain Thomas can't spell while you misspell Edison. Take the time to get your facts straight.

Second, pay attention to tone. Be polite, respectful, kind, and moderate. Fiery sermons work only rarely—no matter what the offense, you usually regret them. Handle criticism with special attention—you don't really want to be remembered a century from now as the one who called Thomas Edison "addled," do you? As you write your draft, delete derogatory references to little Thomas. We don't need to hear that he's only a "little better" in math and science. If he's doing well in them, simply say that. Here's your letter to Mrs. Edison:

Mr. A. Smith

Port Huron Union School

Michigan

March 3, 1854

Mrs. Nancy Edison

Port Huron

Dear Mrs. Edison,

I'm writing to let you know that Thomas has been having difficulty in school this term. While Thomas works well in mathematics and science, his lack of attention has become a problem. Thomas's teachers report that he spends most of his time daydreaming. When asked one day what he was thinking about, Thomas replied that he was "imagining things." We at the Port Huron Union School value creativity. However, Thomas's lack of focus is impeding his studies.

Just last week, Thomas spent a morning fiddling with the school's gas lamp rather than practicing his penmanship, which is very poor. As a result of this continued lack of attention, Thomas does not know his history, has not memorized his poetry when called on to recite, cannot name the states of the Union, and is an exceedingly poor speller.

Thomas's teacher and I would both like to work with you on helping Thomas better focus in the classroom. We could meet at any time during school hours to further discuss ways of motivating your son. Together, I am sure that we can make him a champion speller and a success in life.

Sincerely,

Mr. A. Smith

Principal

CHAPTER 6

BASIC REPORTS

Information-dense reports challenge writers because they're full of so many facts that need organizing. While a report's content might be more complex than what you'll find in a simple letter or e-mail, the structure underneath it remains the same. In this chapter, then, you'll use the Target Outline System to tackle the greater depth a report requires. You'll learn how to use your preliminary notes to spur deeper thought on a subject, and how to write for maximum power.

Of the more complicated forms of business writing, including performance reviews, audits, and proposals, reports are the easiest to tackle. Though more information-dense than brief pieces like memos and letters, they still rely more on facts than persuasion to get their point across.

Reports come in many formats: extended memos, annual reviews, technical reports, audits, progress reports, investigative reports, reports of findings. All have the same basic intent. Reports also require a significant amount of research and extra thought, especially when it comes to making recommendations. Watch how our notes evolve in this chapter as we take on these additional tasks.

Intent: The intent of a report is to:

- Make the reader recognize a problem
- Provide information on a company, project, or process
- Track the progress of a company, project, or person
- Make recommendations

Some reports serve only one of these functions; many serve more than one.

Bottom Line: The bottom line of a report is to:

- Convey information

It can also:

- Get the reader to take an action

The System in 10 Easy Steps

Imagine you're an auditor hired by Spendthrift Incorporated. The company wants you to look at its financial management practices and make recommendations as to how it can improve them. As part of your larger review, you're updating management with a short report on the company's cash disbursement process.

Step 1: Questions and Research

1. **Who is my audience?** Spendthrift management
2. **What do they want to know?** What did you find in your audit? How can I improve my financial management?
3. **What is my bottom line point?** (see below)

Find out (through interviews, observation, document review, and tests):

- Spendthrift's organizational structure
- Spendthrift's current financial policies and processes
- Whether those policies/processes are followed "on the ground"
- Spendthrift's financial and organizational history
- What flaws exist in the system, if any
- What strengths exist, if any
- What Spendthrift's books look like
- What can be done to improve or enhance Spendthrift's system

Step 2: Evaluate Your Notes and Determine the Bottom Line

Here are your preliminary notes:

Spendthrift has three cash accounts: its operating account, used for administrative activity, paying bills, and purchasing products; its investment account; and its payroll account.

We interviewed fifteen managers.

We interviewed four vice presidents.

We tested a sample of funds disbursed from May 1 to July 30, reviewing their supporting documents and authorization.

We reviewed banks statements from January to June 2006.

We documented business processes, identifying risk and controls.

We reviewed the company's policies and procedures for accounting.

Spendthrift's cash disbursement is decentralized. It has an Accounting Department, but Accounting doesn't control cash disbursements.

Everyone from managers and above have access to the check stock and signatory authority to disburse funds on behalf of the company.

They can disburse up to $50,000 without higher authorization—policy 1A47. Anything $50,000 or above requires an authorization from a vice president.

Managers disbursing funds on behalf of the company are required to submit a written requisition with appropriate backup. Our review showed that employees often fail to submit this paperwork.

Spendthrift's bank statements are received in the administrative office and filed by the clerk. We noted that no one performed a bank reconciliation. Upon review, we noted several large discrepancies between the cash accounts per the books and the bank statements. These could not readily be explained by management.

Spendthrift does not have an appropriate segregation of duties. Almost anyone can write large checks, and, without safeguards to prevent it, employees could easily be taking money from the company.

Spendthrift is also at risk for errors in its accounts. Without proper reconciliation, management won't know how much they really have. They might have unaccounted expenditures, overdrafts, or undetected fraudulent activity.

Yikes! What's the bottom line? Spendthrift has pretty much everybody handing out wads of cash, and no one's looking over anyone else's shoulder. Accounting 101 would tell you they're in big trouble. In answer to the question "What did you find?" you've got bad news: You've found that Spendthrift is at risk for major bank overdrafts and possibly fraud—who knows if one of its employees is on a Hawaiian vacation right now, at the company's expense?

This answers the reader's general question, but once you answer it this way, it's not hard to imagine that his very next concern will be minimizing risk. Therefore, if it's within the scope of your report, you'd offer recommendations. Look further at your notes:

Recommendations:

Spendthrift needs to segregate employees' duties. Only the accounting department should be disbursing funds.

At the same time, accounting must be unable to approve a request for funds; otherwise employees could request and approve their own expenditures, and could be spending the company's money on inappropriate or fraudulent purchases.

Before checks are disbursed, Accounting needs to check that there is appropriate backup and authorization for an expenditure.

Spendthrift also must begin reconciling its bank accounts to its general ledger so Accounting can see what is actually leaving the accounts and if they are legitimate expenses. This would be done by those in the Accounting Department who would not have access to disbursed funds.

Now what's the bottom line here? You've got lots of information and several recommendations. You might think you've got more than one Problem—general Accounting doesn't seem to be doing its job, and the other departments are sloppy in keeping track of what they spend. And you've got more than one Resolution—segregation of duties so the people who spend don't also approve their own requests, and reconciliation of accounts.

Don't fall into the trap of thinking you've got more than one overall Problem and Resolution, however. Look for the point that connects them. In order to keep the reader focused, you need to focus yourself—on *one* overall Problem and *one* overall Resolution. This doesn't mean there won't be many elements that fall under that one. But details come later. Look first at the big picture.

What the two Problems you've identified have in common is the failure to control the company's funds. No one knows who's spending what for what. That's where everyone is getting into trouble. Hence, your Problem.

What do all your recommendations have in common? They're about putting a system in place to control and review expenditures. Thus, your Resolution.

The bottom line? Spendthrift can reduce its risk by putting in place a system to control its funds.

You have answered Question 3. You've got a bottom line point that addresses your reader's need. It's time to begin writing.

Step 3: Identify the Problem and Resolution

Spendthrift offers a good example of how identifying the right Problem can make all the difference. Pick the right Problem and you have the reader's attention. Pick the wrong one and you lose it. In this case, if you're the accountant hired to review Spendthrift's books and you found they have multiple, unreconciled accounts, you see an obvious Problem. Why not put it this way: "In our review, we found that Spendthrift Inc. does not reconcile its accounts each month."

Why not? Because that's a Problem to you, but it's clearly not one to your reader. The people at Spendthrift have been doing it that way for years. It doesn't seem to worry them. Risk, however, worries them.

Look to what will interest your reader, and you'll come up with something more like this: "In our review, we found practices that put Spendthrift Corporation at financial risk."

Though he's no accountant, our Spendthrift reader will certainly sit up and take notice of the word "risk." And immediately, he'll start asking questions that move him in the right direction: What's our risk? How can we minimize it?

Now you've got him headed straight toward your answer.

You say:	The reader says:
Problem: Spendthrift faces risk.	*Oh no! Why? How? How can I protect myself?*
Development 1:	
Development 2:	
Development 3:	
Resolution: Spendthrift needs a system to control its funds.	

Step 4: Categorize Your Notes

Spendthrift has three cash accounts: its operating account, used for administrative activity, paying bills, and purchasing products; its investment account; and its payroll account. **COMPANY ACCOUNTS**

We interviewed fifteen managers. **OUR METHODOLOGY**

We interviewed four vice presidents. **OUR METHODOLOGY**

We tested a sample of funds disbursed from May 1 to July 30, reviewing their supporting documents and authorization. **OUR METHODOLOGY**

We reviewed banks statements from January to June 2006. **OUR METHODOLOGY**

We documented business processes, identifying inherent risk and controls. **OUR METHODOLOGY**

We reviewed the company's policies and procedures for accounting. **OUR METHODOLOGY**

Spendthrift's cash disbursement is decentralized. It has an Accounting Department, but Accounting doesn't control cash disbursements. **CASH DISBURSEMENT PROCESS**

Everyone from managers and above have access to the check stock and signatory authority to disburse funds on behalf of the company. **CASH DISBURSEMENT PROCESS**

They can disburse up to $50,000 without higher authorization—policy 1A47. Anything $50,000 or above requires an authorization from a vice president. **CASH DISBURSEMENT PROCESS**

Managers disbursing funds on behalf of the company are required to submit a written requisition with appropriate backup. Our review showed that employees often fail to submit this paperwork. **CASH DISBURSEMENT PROCESS**

Spendthrift's bank statements are received in the administrative office and filed by the clerk. We noted that no one performed a bank rec-onciliation. Upon review, we noted several large discrepancies be-tween the cash accounts per the books and the bank statements. These could not readily be explained by management. **ACCOUNT RECONCILIATION**

Spendthrift does not have an appropriate segregation of duties. Almost anyone can write large checks, and, without safeguards to prevent it, employees could easily be taking money from the company. **RISK**

Spendthrift is also at risk for errors in its accounts. Without proper reconciliation, management won't know how much they really have. They might have unaccounted expenditures, overdrafts, or fraudu-lent activity. **RISK**

Recommendations:

Spendthrift needs to segregate employees' duties. Only the Accounting Department should be disbursing funds. **RECOMMENDATION**

At the same time, Accounting must be unable to approve a request for funds, otherwise employees could request and approve their own expenditures, and could be spending the company's money on inap-propriate or fraudulent purchases. **RECOMMENDATION**

Before checks are disbursed, Accounting needs to check that there is appropriate backup and authorization for an expenditure. **REC-OMMENDATION**

Spendthrift also must begin reconciling its bank accounts to its general ledger so Accounting can see what is actually leaving the accounts and if they are legitimate expenses. This would be done by those in the Accounting Department who would not have access to dis-bursed funds. **RECOMMENDATION**

Again, there's nothing fancy about how we labeled each piece, but instead of sixteen pieces of information, we've now got six categories:

COMPANY ACCOUNTS

OUR METHODOLOGY

CASH DISBURSEMENT PROCESS

ACCOUNT RECONCILIATION

RISK

RECOMMENDATION

Using these categories, it's time to choose the point of insight—the idea that will let the reader make the leap to our Resolution.

Step 5: Choose Development 3—Point of Insight

Which of the categories seems most likely to convince our reader that Spendthrift really needs a system to minimize its risk? The risk itself—most obviously, the risk of fraud.

Why? Because once the reader sees that he is at risk—that people could be stealing large sums from his company's accounts—he realizes that change is imperative. Only then will he be primed for your recommendations.

Therefore, the bottom line of Development 3, the Point of Insight, will be something like: Spendthrift risks fraud.

Now the outline will look like this:

You say:

Problem: Spendthrift faces risk.

Development 1:

Development 2:

Development 3: Spendthrift

  risks fraud.

Resolution: Spendthrift needs a

  system to control its funds.

The reader says:

Oh no! Why? How? How can I

  protect myself?

Uh oh. I can see that. I need help!

  What do I do?

Great idea—sign me up!

Step 6: Choose Development 1—Background

What background must the reader understand in order to launch him into this topic? First, let's see what background we have. What is the crucial context our reader will need to understand and—equally important—accept our conclusions? That will be the methodology, certainly. If he doesn't see what we did, and that we were thorough in our research, he might not believe our findings.

So what goes into our background section? The category OUR METHODOLOGY. What bottom line does it boil down to? The idea that our review has been very thorough—we studied everything, so the reader can trust what we found. Our outline would now look like this:

You say:	*The reader says:*
Problem: Spendthrift faces risk.	*Oh no! Why? How?*
	How can I protect myself?
Development 1: Our methodol-	*You certainly did a thorough*
ogy yields reliable results.	*job. So what did you find?*
Development 2:	
Development 3: Spendthrift	*Uh oh. I can see that. I need help!*
risks fraud.	*What do I do?*
Resolution: Spendthrift needs	*Great idea—sign me up!*
a system to control its funds.	

Step 7: Choose Development 2—Bridge

Finally, what does the reader still need to know? He needs to see what you found after all that review. Only then can he see why he's at risk. What categories in our notes apply? The categories labeled COMPANY ACCOUNTS, CASH DISBURSEMENT PROCESS, and ACCOUNT RECONCILIATION.

The bottom line of all these findings is that they reveal plenty of trouble.

You say:	The reader says:
Problem: Spendthrift faces risk.	*Oh no! Why? How? How can I protect myself?*
Development 1: Our methodology yields reliable results.	*You certainly did a thorough job. So what did you find?*
Development 2: Findings reveal problems.	*Wow. This isn't good, is it?*
Development 3: Spendthrift risks fraud.	*Uh oh. I can see that. I need help! What do I do?*
Resolution: Spendthrift needs a system to control its funds.	*Great idea—sign me up!*

Step 8: Create a List Outline—Organize Categories and Details

First create the List Outline with the categories you have:

Problem: Spendthrift faces risk.

Development 1: Our methodology yields reliable results.

Development 2: Findings reveal problems.

Development 3: Spendthrift risks fraud.

Resolution: Spendthrift needs a system to control its funds.

Problem: Spendthrift faces risk.

METHODOLOGY

Development 1 (Background): Our methodology yields reliable results.

```
┌─────────────────────────────────────────────────────┐
│              CASH DISBURSEMENT PROCESS                │
│              ACCOUNT RECONCILIATION                   │
│              COMPANY ACCOUNTS                         │
└─────────────────────────────────────────────────────┘
                        ⬇
```

Development 2 (Bridge): Findings reveal problems.

```
┌─────────────────────────────────────────────────────┐
│                      RISKS                            │
└─────────────────────────────────────────────────────┘
                        ⬇
```

Development 3 (Point of Insight): Spendthrift risks fraud.

```
┌─────────────────────────────────────────────────────┐
│                 RECOMMENDATIONS                       │
└─────────────────────────────────────────────────────┘
                        ⬇
```

Resolution: Spendthrift needs a system to control its funds.

Notes: Notice again that you've got an empty Problem chunk. In a report, this would be the place to introduce the topic, remind your Spendthrift reader that he hired you to perform this review, and note that below he will see your findings.

A short report will open with nothing more than a subject line, for example, "Subject: Review of Spendthrift Corporation financial management." Either way, the crucial thing is to end with the point of the Problem: You've found Spendthrift is exposing itself to significant risk.

Again, this is not the time to worry about polish. Focus on the organization of the details, not the fine-tuning. So, in a general way, fill in the Problem chunk before you go on:

```
┌─────────────────────────────────────────────────────┐
│  Subject line                                         │
│  Statement of assignment                              │
│  Overall finding that Spendthrift is at financial risk.│
└─────────────────────────────────────────────────────┘
                        ⬇
```

Problem: Spendthrift faces risk.

Next, look at the chunks that have more than one category of notes. In this case, that's only Development 2. Which comes first? Which last? Decide on the order, again, based on logic. You might organize the findings chronologically, if that makes the most sense. But usually, group by subject. Most of all, *decide*. Understand your own logic; don't just throw down a fact because you happened to find a note about it on the top of the stack on your desk.

In our bridge Development, the information that the company keeps three cash accounts must come first, as that's crucial background needed to understand the rest of the review. Which comes next? The cash disbursement process or the fact that the company doesn't reconcile its accounts?

That's a judgment call, but I would argue that account reconciliation should be last, because even with the sloppy process Spendthrift has for disbursing cash, checking the accounts against the general ledger could alert the company to fraud. As it stands, they're missing that important check.

So reorder your Development 2, and it'll look this way:

COMPANY ACCOUNTS
CASH DISBURSEMENT PROCESS
ACCOUNT RECONCILIATION

Development 2 (Bridge): Findings reveal problems.

Once you've set general categories in order, it's time to break out the real notes and begin the more intricate job of organizing them. The principles of the Target Outline continue to apply. Begin with necessary context and move logically toward the bottom line point. Make sure each statement you make, each finding you present, is relevant to that bottom line. You might have discovered along the way that Spendthrift was not the company's original name. At its founding it was Generosity, Inc. Relevant? No. Leave it out.

Now look at your List Outline with notes inside:

Problem: Spendthrift faces risk.

Development 1: Our methodology yields reliable results.

Development 2: Findings reveal problems.

Development 3: Spendthrift risks fraud.

Resolution: Spendthrift needs a system to control its funds.

> Subject line
> Statement of assignment
> Overall finding that Spendthrift is at financial risk.

Problem: Spendthrift faces risk.

> We interviewed fifteen managers.
> We interviewed four vice presidents.
> We tested a sample of funds disbursed from May 1 to July 30, reviewing their supporting documents and authorization.
> We reviewed banks statements from January to June 2006.
> We documented business processes, identifying inherent risk and controls.
> We reviewed the company's policies and procedures for accounting.

Development 1 (Background) Our methodology yields reliable results.

Spendthrift has three cash accounts:

Operating account, used for administrative activity, paying bills and purchasing products;

Investment account;

Payroll account.

Spendthrift's cash disbursement is decentralized. It has an Accounting Department, but Accounting doesn't control cash disbursements.

Everyone from managers and above have access to check stock and signatory authority.

Managers and above can disburse up to $50,000 without higher authorization—policy 1A47.

$50,000 and above requires authorization from a vice president.

Managers disbursing funds on behalf of the company are required to submit a written requisition with appropriate backup. Our review showed that employees often fail to submit this paperwork.

Spendthrift's bank statements are received in the administrative office and filed by the clerk. We noted that no one performed a bank reconciliation.

Upon review, we noted several large discrepancies between the cash accounts per the books and the bank statements.

These could not readily be explained by management.

Development 2 (Bridge): Findings reveal problems.

Spendthrift does not have segregation of duties. Therefore, it is at risk for errors in its accounts.

Almost anyone can write large checks, and, without safeguards to prevent it, employees could easily be taking money from the company.

Without proper reconciliation, no one knows how much the company has. This puts the company at risk for unaccounted expenditures, overdrafts, and possible fraudulent activity.

Development 3 (Point of Insight): Spendthrift risks fraud.

Recommendations:

Spendthrift should segregate employees' duties. Only the Accounting Department should be disbursing funds.

At the same time, Accounting must be unable to approve a request for funds, to avoid employees requesting and granting their own expenditures, spending the company's funds inappropriately, or making fraudulent purchases.

Accounting should check for appropriate backup and authorization before disbursing checks.

Spendthrift must begin reconciling its bank accounts to its general ledger, so Accounting can determine expenditures are legitimate.

Those reconciling accounts should have no access to disbursed funds.

Resolution: Spendthrift needs a system to control its funds.

Notice that as I organized my notes, I smoothed them out little by little. They're not exactly polished, but they're one step closer to finished text.

Step 9: Add Transitions and an Opening Hook

Transitions in our Spendthrift audit are still simple, and will mostly be taken care of with headings. Notice some transitions appear naturally in our notes. For example, in Development 3, we write, "Therefore, it is at risk for errors in its accounts," which connects the idea of Spendthrift's failure to segregate duties with the risks it causes.

Here, the opening hook is as simple as a subject line.

Step 10: Polish Your Draft

The two main issues when it comes to polishing this draft will be formatting and tone. Technical material will require good use of formatting, plenty of bullets, headings, and white space, to help the reader absorb the details. Look at how adding bullets and headings helps our Recommendations section:

Before

To protect against fraudulent use of funds and inappropriate purchases, we recommend a segregation of duties. In regard to fund disbursement, we recommend giving the Accounting Department sole responsibility for disbursing funds. As part of its enhanced role, Accounting should be unable to approve funding requests. Spendthrift should also require Accounting to check for appropriate backup and authorization of purchases before disbursing funds.

In addition, Accounting should be responsible for reconciling the company's accounts. In this capacity, it should reconcile Spendthrift's bank accounts to its general ledger and segregate the duties of those reconciling the accounts from those disbursing funds or receiving payments.

After

Recommendations

To protect against fraudulent use of funds and inappropriate purchases, we recommend a segregation of duties:

Fund Disbursement

- Give the Accounting Department sole ability to disburse funds
- Bar Accounting from approving funding requests
- Institute a requirement that Accounting check for appropriate backup and authorization of purchases before disbursing funds

Bank Reconciliation

Accounting should also be responsible for reconciling the company's accounts. It should:

- Reconcile Spendthrift's bank accounts to its general ledger
- Segregate the duties of those reconciling the accounts from those disbursing funds or receiving payments

Tone is also crucial in a document like this one, because you are the expert reporting to a client. Remember that your client doesn't necessarily realize the dangers of keeping three accounts and not reconciling them. You must sound professional and serious, not alarmist. Avoid jargon, but also refrain from being too colloquial.

(opening hook)

From: Consultants LLP

To: Spendthrift, Inc.

Date: May 1, 2007

Subject: Review of Spendthrift Incorporated accounting practices

Spendthrift, Inc., engaged Consultants LLP to perform a review of its accounting processes for managing risk and controlling accounts. The results of our review found that Spendthrift's current process for disbursing funds puts the company at significant financial risk.

PROBLEM: SPENDTHRIFT FACES RISK.

<u>Background</u> (transition)

Consultants LLP reviewed Spendthrift's systems for disbursing funds and reconciling its cash accounts. In the course of our review, we:

• Interviewed key personnel to determine how they disbursed funds and tracked expenditures (including fifteen managers and four vice presidents)

• Reviewed the company's policies and procedures for key accounting processes

• Documented business processes, identifying risk and controls

• Tested a sample of funds disbursed from May 1 to July 30, 2006, including appropriate supporting documents and authorization

• Reviewed bank statements from January to June 2006

DEVELOPMENT 1: OUR METHODOLOGY YIELDS RELIABLE RESULTS.

<u>Findings</u> (transition)

Disbursement of Funds **(transition)**

Spendthrift has three cash accounts:

- An operating account for administrative activity, paying bills, and purchasing products
- An investment account
- A payroll account

Although Spendthrift has an Accounting Department, Accounting currently does not control all cash disbursement. Instead, Spendthrift authorizes managers in any department to spend as they deem appropriate on behalf of the company. Managers have access to check stock and signatory authority, and per policy 1A47, they can disburse up to $50,000 without authorization. To write a check above that amount, the policy requires that managers receive authorization from a vice president; however, we noted no control in place to monitor this.

Spendthrift policy requires managers disbursing funds on the company's behalf to submit a written requisition form with appropriate backup to justify their request. However, our review showed that employees often fail to submit this paperwork.

Bank Reconciliation **(transition)**

Spendthrift's bank statements are received in the administrative office and filed by a clerk. We noted that no one performs a bank reconciliation. Upon review, we found several large discrepancies between the cash accounts, as recorded in the company's ledger, and the bank statements. These could not readily be explained by management.

DEVELOPMENT 2: FINDINGS REVEAL PROBLEMS.

Observations **(transition)**

Spendthrift does not currently segregate duties between those who approve requisitions and payment and those authorized to write checks. Managers from any department can write checks in any amount, without safeguards to prevent or detect misuse of funds. Without these necessary internal controls, the company puts itself at risk of fraud.

In addition **(transition)**, without reconciling accounts, Accounting cannot verify that the bank account accurately reflects deposits and disbursements, or verify the accuracy of cash balances in the ledger. This puts the company at risk for unaccounted expenditures, overdrafts, and fraudulent activity.

DEVELOPMENT 3: SPENDTHRIFT RISKS FRAUD.

Recommendations **(transition)**

To protect against both inappropriate purchases and fraud, we recommend a segregation of duties:

Fund Disbursement **(transition)**

• Give the Accounting Department sole authority to disburse funds.

• Bar Accounting from approving requisitions.

• Institute a requirement that Accounting review all expenditures for appropriate backup and authorization prior to disbursing funds.

Bank Reconciliation **(transition)**

Accounting should also be responsible for reconciling the company's accounts monthly. It should:

• Reconcile Spendthrift's bank accounts to the general ledger.

• Segregate the duties of those reconciling the account from those disbursing funds or receiving payments.

Thank you for your cooperation and help during this audit. We appreciate the opportunity to work with Spendthrift. If you have any questions about any part of this review, please contact John Doe at 555-555-5555.

RESOLUTION: SPENDTHRIFT NEEDS A SYSTEM TO CONTROL ITS FUNDS.

A NOTE ON INFORMATION-ONLY REPORTS

What if your reader doesn't want recommendations, but only hopes to learn about a product or system? How can you make a point when your bottom line is simply to provide information? The point of an information-only report is to educate the reader. In that case, you want the reader asking questions like the following: "What is this? What does it involve? How is it made? How does it work? What is its history? What is its future?" Simple, broad Problem statements prompt questions like these. For example: "Roller coasters rely on basic physics to provide a heart-pumping thrill." (The reader asks: How do they work?)

The Resolution of such a report requires that the reader understand the system or product. Our roller coaster Resolution, for example, might read: "Modern roller coasters rely on the same basic technology as those of old: They use track design to build up energy and release it in heart-stopping plunges." The journey to that Resolution should have taught the reader the physics behind roller coasters, how coasters are built, and how they're run.

To organize an information-only report, first rely on chronology. What must the reader know first? What next? The point of insight will always be the idea or fact that, in the end, makes the product or system work. While our roller coaster report might offer a background section on basic physics and a bridge on how designers start and stop the coaster, the point of insight will be track design, which is what produces that distinctive coaster thrill.

To take another example, in a report on the theme park industry, your reader might want to know what's involved in opening and running a park. The Developments would introduce him to all the elements of a theme park: the different rides, food courts, and arcades that make up the amusements; the regulations that govern safety; the maintenance needed to keep a park safe; and the overall management required to see that the park runs smoothly. Since in this case the Problem statement merely introduces all the aspects of the subject, the Resolution in such a report could simply reiterate it. This time, however, the reader's no longer asking a question. He reads the Resolution's sum-up and says—yes, now I know what you mean.

Our theme park report outline might look like this:

You say:	The reader says:
Problem: Theme parks require unifying vision, consistent maintenance, and strong management.	*What does each involve?*
Development 1 (Background): Theme defines rides, games, and food areas.	*I understand.*
Development 2 (Bridge): Parks require regular maintenance.	*I can see the importance of that.*
Development 3 (Point of Insight): Management keeps park running.	*That's the most important element!*
Resolution: Parks require vision, maintenance, and management.	*I can see that!*

Here, the point of insight provides less a feeling of *aha!* than a growing, nearly complete understanding of the subject. By the Resolution, the reader should walk away satisfied that he has learned—which is the reason he picked up your report in the first place.

CHAPTER 7

PERFORMANCE EVALUATIONS

Performance evaluations are no one's favorite job. Many companies offer forms to fill in for personnel evaluations, but whether you're filling in the blanks or creating your own performance evaluation, you need to know how to craft your message. Performance evaluations are delicate, because they often require that you point out weaknesses in a project or employee. How exactly to frame these weaknesses depends, as always, on your bottom line.

Intent: The intent of a performance evaluation is to:

- Track the progress of a person or project
- Delineate the person's responsibilities/the project's scope
- Explore the skills of the person or people involved
- Explore the weaknesses of the person/people/project
- Make recommendations as to promotions/future steps

Evaluations can do all or only a few of these jobs, depending on their scope.

Bottom Line: The bottom line of a performance evaluation is to answer the question, How is this person or project doing? Can it/he/she do better? Is it/he/she ready for the next step/level of responsibility?

The System in 10 Easy Steps

The young barbarian Attila the Hun is coming up for review by horde leaders. Is he ready for a greater leadership role? As you're his direct supervisor—just above him in the Hun organization—it's your job to evaluate his performance this past year.

Step 1: Questions and Research

1. **Who is my audience?** The head Hun. However, it's also Attila, who will get a copy of his evaluation. Make sure you don't put anything in this evaluation that you wouldn't say directly to Attila (and expect to live).
2. **What does he want to know?** How is Attila doing on the job? What are his strengths and weaknesses? Is he ready for more responsibility?
3. **What is my bottom line point?** (see below)

Find out:

- Attila's responsibilities
- Attila's skills
- How he has performed on the job (with specific examples)
- What weaknesses he shows
- What strengths he shows
- What you ought to recommend, given his performance

Step 2: Evaluate Your Notes and Determine the Bottom Line

Anyone who's read Wess Roberts's *Leadership Secrets of Attila the Hun* knows Attila turned into quite a leader. But what was he like as a low-level barbarian? A cog in the Hun organization? What do we know about his work? Let's, with apologies to historians, go find out. Interview some of his fellow barbarians, observe him on the job, see how good he is at sacking and pillaging. Take a look at your notes:

As a member of the horde, Attila is responsible for taking part in raids and hunts. As part of the royal family, he is also occasionally called on to lead small hordes, of 30 or so Huns.

In battle, his main objective is to kill as many as possible, and to take no prisoners. Attila also is responsible for gathering booty.

Attila has taken part in three raids this year—one of the Visigoths, two on the outskirts of Rome's Western Empire.

He's also led the hunt twice this quarter, bringing down a bear and two wolves.

Attila is strong and hearty. He's an expert horseman. He brought the bear down while atop his horse, disemboweled it, and ate it raw.

Attila shows great potential as a leader. He inspires real fear in everyone around him. Even his brother, Brela, confesses to fearing him. Brela sleeps with one eye open when Attila is around.

On the Visigoth raid, Attila showed initiative. Not only did he plunder the city, he also adorned its gates with a spike topped by the Visigoth general's head.

Attila's profit margin this year has been high. He plundered seven gold bowls and three pots of foodstuffs from the Visigoths.

Attila has mastered the use of weaponry. He's able to wield a club, short dagger, sword, and spear with equal skill.

Attila is an equal opportunity pillager. In our recent attack on the Western Roman Empire, Attila attacked Visigoths, Romans, and even monks in the monastery. That kind of multiculturalism will take him far as a barbarian.

Attila's experience as a child hostage in the Roman court gives him knowledge of the enemy's customs and strategy.

Attila knows the value of a good bribe. He's already successfully ex-
tracted gold tribute from some provinces in the Eastern Empire, in
exchange for letting them live.

Attila has a weakness for drink and women. He has several hundred
wives already and has been known to fall asleep in a drunken stu-
por, leaving him vulnerable to enemies.

The worst example of this came on his 252nd wedding night, when he
drank so much he fell asleep among the horses and was nearly
smothered under his favorite mare.

The bottom line? Attila looks like pretty good management material. Despite his weakness for wine and women, he's strong, cunning, and, best of all, ambitious. So the bottom line? Attila deserves a promotion.

Step 3: Identify the Problem and Resolution

If the answer you want to provide is that Attila deserves a promotion, what's the question you want the reader asking? It's—How did Attila perform this year?

Prompt him to ask that with something simple like: The following is a review of Attila the Hun's performance for the year 424. In other words, it's the idea that I, the reviewer, performed a review. Naturally, the reader will want to know how Attila did.

You say:	The reader says:
Problem: I review Attila.	*How did Attila perform this year?*
Development 1:	
Development 2:	
Development 3:	
Resolution: Attila deserves a **promotion.**	*He certainly does!*

Step 4: Categorize Your Notes

As a member of the horde, Attila is responsible for taking part in raids and hunts. As part of the royal family, he is also occasionally called on to lead small hordes, of 30 or so Huns. **RESPONSIBILITIES**

In battle, his main objective is to kill as many as possible and to take no prisoners. Attila also is responsible for gathering booty. **RESPONSIBILITIES**

Attila has taken part in three raids this year—one of the Visigoths, two on the outskirts of Rome's Western Empire. **BATTLE EXPERIENCE**

He's also led the hunt twice this quarter, bringing down a bear and two wolves. **SKILL**

Attila is strong and hearty. He's an expert horseman. He brought the bear down while atop his horse, disemboweled it, and ate it raw. **SKILL, HEALTH**

Attila shows great potential as a leader. He inspires real fear in everyone around him. Even his brother, Brela, confesses to fearing him. Brela sleeps with one eye open when Attila is around. **LEADERSHIP POTENTIAL**

On the Visigoth raid, Attila showed initiative. Not only did he plunder the city, he also adorned its gates with a spike topped by the Visigoth general's head. **EXAMPLE OF LEADERSHIP**

Attila's profit margin this year has been high. He plundered seven gold bowls and three pots of foodstuffs from the Visigoths. **PROFIT**

Attila has mastered the use of weaponry. He's able to wield a club, short dagger, sword, and spear with equal skill. **SKILL**

Attila is an equal opportunity pillager. In our recent attack on the Western Roman Empire, Attila attacked Visigoths, Romans, and even monks in the monastery. That kind of multiculturalism will take him far as a barbarian. **LEADERSHIP POTENTIAL**

Attila's experience as a child hostage in the Roman court gives him knowledge of the enemy's customs and strategy. **EXPERTISE**

Attila knows the value of a good bribe. He's already successfully extracted gold tribute from some provinces in the Eastern Empire in exchange for letting them live. **EXAMPLE OF LEADERSHIP, PROFIT**

Attila has a weakness for drink and women. He has several hundred wives already and has been known to fall asleep in a drunken stupor, leaving him vulnerable to enemies. **WEAKNESS**

The worst example of this came on his 252nd wedding night, when he drank so much he fell asleep among the horses and was nearly smothered under his favorite mare. **WEAKNESS**

Our categories now boil down to:

RESPONSIBILITIES
BATTLE EXPERIENCE
SKILL
HEALTH
LEADERSHIP POTENTIAL
EXAMPLE OF LEADERSHIP
PROFIT
EXPERTISE
WEAKNESS

Step 5: Choose Development 3—Point of Insight

Already, you can see that our Attila evaluation is more complex than our Spendthrift report, because our notes are harder to categorize. Some of the areas seem to overlap, and one or two are labeled twice. That's fine. You handle that added layer of complexity by tackling the obvious first.

Which category will best show that Attila is leadership material? Both LEADERSHIP POTENTIAL and the EXAMPLE we have of Attila's leadership—his participation in raids, including conquering the Visigoth village—would serve us well. So would the fact that Attila has already benefited the organization, by bringing in plunder (our PROFIT category). Label them all D3. Now, which will we turn into the bottom line of that Development and which will become a List point in the chunk?

To determine that, ask yourself which is more powerful, potential or proof? Proof trumps potential every time. Next, ask yourself which proof is more compelling, the fact that he brought out plunder or the innovation of spearing the Visigoth general's head?

Again, put yourself in the mind of the reader. The Visigoth-head-on-a-spike stunt is a nice bit of terrorist theater, but most organizations come down, in the end, to dollars and cents. Therefore, let's make PROFIT the bottom line of Development 3, the reader's Point of Insight.

Remember that Attila's potential and his Visigoth adventure will both appear in Development 3. But the chunk will end with our strongest point—that he's already turning that potential into reality.

Now our outline looks like this:

You say:	The reader says:
Problem: I review Attila.	*How did Attila perform this year?*
Development 1:	
Development 2:	
Development 3: Profit shows leadership.	*Attila's filling our coffers? I'm impressed!*
Resolution: Attila deserves a promotion.	*He certainly does!*

Step 6: Choose Development 1—Background

Next comes Development 1, our background Development. Look at the categories again:

RESPONSIBLITIES

BATTLE EXPERIENCE **D3**

SKILL

HEALTH

LEADERSHIP POTENTIAL **D3**

EXAMPLE OF LEADERSHIP **D3**

PROFIT **D3**

EXPERTISE

WEAKNESS

Which among our categories belongs in our first Development? Here's where this piece gets trickier. Is the background Attila's responsibilities or the fact that he's skilled in the ways of barbarism? Is it that he's physically fit? Or perhaps we should deal first with his weaknesses, so we can move on to his strengths?

To make this decision, return to the most basic principle of writing: it's all about the reader. What point do you want to remain in your reader's mind once he's done reading? You want him to remember that Attila is ready for promotion. Evaluate the options with that in mind. His skills relate to his expertise as a warrior, and that category is also closely tied to leadership. Therefore, it will probably end up in the Bridge Development, D2, where it can lead directly into how he's *using* those skills. That leaves Attila's responsibilities and his weaknesses. Responsibilities certainly belong in Development 1—they're necessary background. If we don't know what is expected of our barbarian, how do we know if he's measuring up?

However, though responsibilities belong in Development 1, are they the bottom line of the whole chunk?

Categorizing and organizing notes takes real thought. It's relatively easy to bunch ideas together, but you must make sure that they make the relevant point— the point that will bolster your overall argument, which is that Attila deserves a promotion. In this case, we need to think about Attila's weaknesses. They're important because if he doesn't correct them, he'll end up a weaker leader. Therefore, Attila's weaknesses are the bottom line of the background Development.

You say:	The reader says:
Problem: I review Attila.	How did Attila perform this year?
Development 1: Weakness requires improvement.	Yes, I can see that Attila could use a little smoothing out of the rough edges.
Development 2:	
Development 3: Profit shows leadership.	Attila's filling our coffers? I'm impressed!
Resolution: Attila deserves a promotion.	He certainly does!

Breathe a sigh of relief. You've communicated the areas Attila needs to improve upon, and you're still alive. Next, to the Bridge, Development 2.

Step 7: Choose Development 2—Bridge

What's left? Look at your notes again:

RESPONSIBILITIES **D1**

BATTLE EXPERIENCE **D3**

SKILL

HEALTH

LEADERSHIP POTENTIAL **D3**

EXAMPLE OF LEADERSHIP **D3**

PROFIT **D3**

EXPERTISE

WEAKNESS **D1**

Attila's skill, health, and expertise are all left, and all of them can be generalized into a bottom line for Development 2: Attila's qualities equip him to lead. One final look at our Target Outline, and we're ready to move on to the List.

You say:		The reader says:
Problem: I review Attila.		*How did Attila perform this year?*
Development 1: Weakness requires improvement.		*Yes, I can see that Attila could use a little smoothing out of the rough edges.*
Development 2: Qualities equip Attila.		*He certainly has what it takes to lead!*
Development 3: Profit shows leadership.		*Attila's filling our coffers? I'm impressed!*
Resolution: Attila deserves a promotion.		*He certainly does!*

Step 8: Create a List Outline—Organize Categories and Details

Create the List Outline first with our categories of notes:

Problem: I review Attila.

Development 1: Weakness requires improvement.

Development 2: Qualities equip Attila.

Development 3: Profit shows leadership.

Resolution: Attila deserves promotion.

The following is a review of Attila the Hun's performance for the year 424.

Problem: I review Attila.

RESPONSIBILITIES
WEAKNESSES

Development 1: Weakness requires improvement.

SKILL
HEALTH
EXPERTISE

Development 2: Qualities equip Attila.

BATTLE EXPERIENCE
LEADERSHIP POTENTIAL
EXAMPLE OF LEADERSHIP
PROFIT

Development 3: Profit shows leadership.

Recommendation for promotion

Resolution: Attila deserves promotion.

Notes: Once categories are in general order, we evaluate. Our Development 2, the Bridge, has three categories: SKILL, HEALTH, and EXPER-

TISE. Is this the correct sequence? HEALTH, which is something Attila can't control, is our weakest point. In writing, power always comes at the end. You want your reader reading from point to point this way: Oh, good point. Interesting. Oh! That makes real sense! OH! Definitely! I'm convinced.

Therefore, HEALTH, our weakest category, should go first. Which comes next, SKILL or EXPERTISE? That's a judgment call. Make a choice, again, based on the reader. In Hun society, it's likely some others can ride a horse and take down a bear. But how many have the added advantage of having been captives among the Romans, learning their ways? EXPERTISE trumps SKILL. Order it that way.

What about Development 3, our reader's Point of Insight? Is it in the right order? Not given our audience. Attila's potential as a leader, seen through his fierceness and the fact that he's an equal opportunity pillager, is nice, but his battle experience shows he can lead, and his innovative terrorizing of the Visigoths shows he's got just the brutal cast of mind that can turn an average barbarian into a great one. Best of all, he's already proven he's a leader by bringing real plunder to the group. Therefore, the order ought to be: LEADERSHIP POTENTIAL, BATTLE EXPERIENCE, EXAMPLE OF LEADERSHIP, and, last, PROFIT.

Now that we've got our order, let's lay out the original notes:

Problem: I review Attila.

Development 1: Weakness requires improvement.

Development 2: Qualities equip Attila.

Development 3: Profit shows leadership.

Resolution: Attila deserves promotion.

The following is a review of Attila the Hun's performance for the year 424.

Problem: I review Attila.

As a member of the horde, Attila is responsible for taking part in raids and hunts.
   As part of the royal family, he is also occasionally called on to lead small hordes,
   of 30 or so Huns.
In battle, his main objective is to kill as many as possible and to take no prisoners.
   Attila also is responsible for gathering booty.
Attila has a weakness for drink and women. He has several hundred wives already
   and has been known to fall asleep in a drunken stupor, leaving him vulnerable
   to enemies.
The worst example of this came on his 252nd wedding night, when he drank so
   much he fell asleep among the horses and was nearly smothered under his favorite mare.

Development 1: Weakness requires improvement.

Attila is strong and hearty.
He's an expert horseman.
He's led the hunt twice this quarter, bringing down a bear and two wolves.
He brought the bear down while atop his horse, disemboweled it, and ate it raw.
Attila has mastered the art of weaponry. He's able to wield a club, short dagger,
   sword, and spear with equal skill.
Attila's experience as a child hostage in the Roman court gives him knowledge of
   the enemy's customs and strategy.

Development 2: Qualities equip Attila.

Attila shows great potential as a leader. He inspires real fear in everyone around him. Even his brother, Brela, confessed to fearing him. Brela sleeps with one eye open when Attila is around.

Attila is an equal opportunity pillager. In our recent attack on the Western Roman Empire, Attila attacked Visigoths, Romans, and even monks in the monastery. That kind of multiculturalism will take him far as a barbarian.

Attila has taken part in three raids this year, one of the Visigoths, and two on the outskirts of Rome's Western Empire.

On the Visigoth raid, Attila showed initiative. Not only did he plunder the city, he also adorned its gates with a spike topped by the Visigoth general's head.

Attila's margin this year has been high. He plundered seven gold bowls and three pots of foodstuffs from the Visigoths.

Attila also knows the value of a good bribe. He's already extracted gold tribute from some provinces in the Eastern Empire in exchange for letting them live.

Development 3: Profit shows leadership.

Recommendation for promotion.

Resolution: Attila deserves promotion.

Step 9: Add Transitions and an Opening Hook

Each section in the performance evaluation requires a small introduction of its own. These, whether set as headings or an opening line, will serve as transitions from one section to the next. The opening hook will be a line labeled "Subject," which gives a brief heading to orient the reader, and a line labeled "Scope," which usually tells the reader the time period covered under the review.

Step 10: Polish Your Draft

Keep in mind that performance reviews have a double audience—both the subject of the review and the manager or higher-up who receives it. Criticism should be constructive and, as long as the overall review is positive, should be couched in terms of how weaknesses can be improved to further strengthen the employee's performance. Even if you're filling in a form, be certain you're making coherent points.

Categories within a performance review can be put together in any number of ways. They may be grouped by responsibilities, by performance on a specific project, or by skills and use of those skills. However you decide to order your Developments—and writing is all about making those decisions—make sure you have clearly thought through your Problem and Resolution, and how each of the Developments relates to your bottom line.

Finally, make use of headings and other formatting, such as bullets and white space, to make the review easy on the eye and allow the reader to scan to the bottom line: the overall positive or negative result of the review.

See below for Attila's draft (Target Outline elements appear in capital letters; List Outline elements are bold and in parentheses):

(opening hook)

To: Chief Hun

From: Middle Manager Hun

Subject: Performance Review, Attila the Hun

Scope: The following is a review of Attila the Hun's performance for the year 424.

PROBLEM: I REVIEW ATTILA.

<u>Responsibilities</u> **(transition)**

As a member of the horde, Attila is responsible for taking part in raids and hunts. As part of the royal family, he is also occasionally called on to lead small hordes, of thirty or so Huns. In battle, Attila's main objective is to kill as many of the enemy as possible and to take no prisoners. Attila is also responsible for gathering booty.

Areas in Need of Improvement (transition)

Overall, Attila is a strong member of the Hun organization with excellent leadership skills. However, Attila has a weakness for drink and women. He has several hundred wives already and has been known to fall asleep in a drunken stupor, leaving him vulnerable to enemies. The worst example of this came on his 252nd wedding night, when he drank so much he fell asleep among the horses and was nearly smothered under his favorite mare. Despite this, Attila's strengths far outweigh his weaknesses.

DEVELOPMENT 1: WEAKNESS REQUIRES IMPROVEMENT.

Strengths (transition)

Attila's skills have earned him a reputation for cunning, strength, and courage. Strong and healthy, he is an excellent horseman and a skilled hunter. He's led the hunt twice this quarter, bringing down a bear and two wolves. He netted the bear while on horseback, disemboweled it, and ate it raw.

Attila has also mastered the art of weaponry. He wields a club, short dagger, sword, and spear with equal skill.

Finally, Attila's experience as a child hostage in the Roman court gives him knowledge of the enemy's customs and strategy.

DEVELOPMENT 2: QUALITIES EQUIP ATTILA.

Leadership Qualities (transition)

Attila shows great potential as a leader. He inspires real fear in everyone around him, including his brother, Brela. Brela confesses to sleeping with one eye open when Attila is around.

In addition, Attila is an equal opportunity pillager. In our recent attack on the Western Roman Empire, Attila attacked Visigoths, Romans, and even monks in the monastery. That kind of multiculturalism will take him far as a barbarian.

Attila has taken part in three raids this year, one of the Visigoths and two on the outskirts of Rome's Western Empire. On the Visigoth raid, Attila showed initiative. Not only did he plunder the city, he also adorned its gates with the Visigoth general's head on a spike.

Attila's profit margin this year has been high. He plundered seven gold bowls and three pots of foodstuffs from the Visigoths. He also knows the value of a good bribe. He extracted a gold tribute from the provinces of Rome's Eastern Empire in exchange for letting the outer villages live.

DEVELOPMENT 3: PROFIT SHOWS LEADERSHIP.

Recommendation (transition)

Attila's ingenuity and courage in the hunt and in battle, his creative strategy for inspiring fear in enemies and in the horde, and the bounty he has brought to the Hun organization all show that Attila is ready to take the next step and assume more responsibility in the Hun organization. We recommend that he receive a promotion to leader of the Eastern Horde.

RESOLUTION: ATTILA DESERVES PROMOTION.

CHAPTER 8
GENERAL PROPOSALS

Proposals are a sales tool. They're meant to persuade the reader that you and your company can provide a service or product better than anyone else. The difficulty when it comes to writing proposals is dealing with your own weaknesses. Everyone has a weakness or two, and both acknowledging them and minimizing the damage they cause is the secret to writing a winning proposal.

Some proposals come in response to a Request for Proposal (RFP). These usually dictate a rigid structure for answering the reader's question. Even in such formal proposals, however, your job is to highlight your strengths and minimize your weaknesses. See the note on page 127 to learn how to do that even in the context of a structure dictated by someone else.

Intent: The intent of a proposal is to:

- Show the reader you understand his or her needs
- Highlight your applicable skills
- Lay out your related experience
- Estimate or provide pricing for your service or product

- Present a plan for providing a service or product
- Show the reader you can provide a service or product better than anyone else

Bottom Line: The bottom line of proposal is to:

- Convince the reader to choose your service or product

The System in 10 Easy Steps

Julius Caesar, recently named dictator for life after many military triumphs, plans to attend a meeting of the Roman Senate on the fifteenth of March, commonly known as the "Ides." As Rome's most popular personality, he'll be cheered along a parade route on his way to the Forum, where the Senate will meet. He's nervous, however, due to several recent security alerts: a soothsayer's warning to "beware the Ides of March"; nightmares that plague his wife, Calpurnia, foretelling his murder; and the worrisome appearance of the entrails of his recent animal sacrifices. Unsure whom he can trust and afraid to appear weak, he has issued a quiet call for proposals from the top security firms in Rome.

You are a partner in Mercenary Security, one of the top five security firms in the republic, and with this proposal, you hope to win one of the plum jobs of the millennia.

Step 1: Questions and Research

1. **Who is my audience?** Julius Caesar, Dictator Perpetuo, Rome
2. **What does he want to know?** Why should I choose you to protect me on the Ides?
3. **What is my bottom line point?** (see below)

Find out:

- What the job entails
- Background on Caesar and the current situation
- Your firm's relevant skills
- Your pricing structure
- Your relevant experience
- What it would take for your company to protect Caesar (your approach to the project)

Step 2: Evaluate Your Notes and Determine the Bottom Line

Heads of state our specialty for 25 years. (We've protected Herod, Cleopatra.)

Herod (3 years ago in Galilee we protected the governor during village tour. Locals rioted, state guards fled, we subdued crowd, beat back rebels, returned Herod and retinue home.)

2 years ago—adjunct security for Cleopatra's birthday celebration in Alexandria. Did parade route security, temple security. Our under-cover priest stuck with Cleopatra during sacrifices. On that job, pre-festival investigation uncovered rebellious cousin plotting assassination—dispatched her early with poisoned dagger made to simulate bite of an asp.

We train with South Britain's Belgic tribes—famous for fierceness and strategic excellence.

We've got daggers, spears, bows, arrows, armor—all from top weapon-smiths in Rome.

We keep it quiet. No one in Alexandria knew we were protecting Cleopatra. People still think her cousin died of snakebite (govern-ment ruled it suicide).

We know what Caesar needs. Investigated soothsayer Spurrina's warning, Calpurnia's dreams, and the bad entrails. Based on evidence, we'll focus on security from midmorning of the Ides through Senate meeting.

Understand the need for secrecy. Senators might have conspired to weaken centurion guard. So (as Caesar advised) we'd make his friend Marcus Brutus security liaison.

We know the rules. Work ends at the Senate door.

Our plan:

Coordinator: Marcus Valerius

Nones March through the Ides, our scouts interview associates and potential rivals, check parade route, secure Senate area.

On the Ides:

Hire first-class fortune-teller to warn us of trouble.

Line parade route with plain-toga security, armed with concealed daggers.

Station our own gladiators (in full armor) around the Forum.

Station expert archers on the rooftop of the Forum buildings.

Employ fleet-footed runners to carry messages from the field to Marcus Valerius (overseeing operation from command center in a corner shop of the Forum).

Plan enables Caesar to be secure while showing strong face to masses. He can publicly dismiss government guard and know we're on the job. Except for Brutus, no one outside of Mercenary Security will know of our involvement.

Breakdown of fees, based on hourly billing rates:

Partner: 1 denarius

2 Scouts: 1 sestertii

1 fortune-teller: 1 sestertii

Gladiators: 1 dupondii

Message runners: 2 copper semisses

Plain-toga security: 1 quinarii

Archers: 3 sestertii

Personal bodyguards: 1 sestertii

Estimated time:

Partner and scouts—one week

Others—Ides, for three hours

Total estimate: 105 denarii (includes margin for out-of-pocket expenses)

We require half in advance.

Fee increases up to 20 percent if we see major combat or if more than one quarter of our men are killed.

"Mercenary guarantee"—lead partner poisons himself if project fails. (Good track record—we're all still here.)

Our motto: primo confuto, deinde caedo furtim, tandem eradico *(first suppress, then kill with stealth, finally crush).*

The bottom line? The bottom line in this case springs from a combination of points. Mercenary has impressive experience, a good set of skills, and a detailed plan for the Ides. Together, these could sell Caesar on our firm. Therefore, the bottom line will be: Our expertise and experience, and most of all our detailed plan, make us the best for this job.

The challenge of this proposal will be twofold, however. Mercenary's pricing is steep, so expensive it might *lose* the company the job. This proposal, then, must convey the cost of the service in a way that does not undercut the sale and, ideally, in a way that enhances the bottom line.

Step 3: Identify the Problem and Resolution

Top proposals take a reader's need and match it to the company's greatest strength. To write a really strong proposal, we must honestly evaluate our own strengths and weaknesses. It helps to make a simple list. Take a look at Mercenary's list:

STRENGTHS

Experience/Success rate—We've worked successfully for several of the big names in the republic (Cleopatra, Herod), and we've been in business for 25 years.

Training—Our people are experts in weapons and skilled in battle.

Plan—We know the field so well we're able to come up with a detailed plan that shows we've thought of everything.

Discretion—We're able to keep things quiet.

WEAKNESSES

We're expensive. Our extensive personnel and heavy cache of weapons requires us to charge more. We cost at least a third more than some of the republic's smaller, local security firms.

What is the common theme in our strengths? Once we figure this out, it will become the theme of our proposal, highlighted in the Problem section and in every transition all the way to the Resolution, where we show Caesar we provide what he needs. In this case, we know Caesar needs protection, but "protection" could mean anything from a few extra bodyguards to a full-strength army. Our strength as a company lies in our proven expertise in just these kinds of situations. Expertise covers all our strengths—we earned it with skill and experience, and we prove it with our detailed plan.

Expertise, then, becomes our proposal's theme, and the job of our Problem section will be to reframe Caesar's simple need—security—into a need for *expert* security. Do that by saying it that way, with something like "Providing discrete security for a head of state requires more than simply weapons and manpower. It requires skill, careful preparation, and a detailed plan.

With over 25 years in the field, Mercenary Security offers just this type of expertise."

Once Caesar sees what we've got to offer, he'll realize that ordering a few extra legionnaires is not going to cover his needs on the Ides. He needs *experts*. And that's what Mercenary Security offers.

You say:		The reader says:
Problem: Caesar needs		*You're right. This is a complicated*
expertise.		*job. But how do I know you're the*
		experts?
Resolution: We provide		*Great—you're hired!*
expertise.		

Step 4: Categorize Your Notes

Heads of state our specialty for 25 years. (We've protected Herod, Cleopatra.) **EXPERIENCE**

Herod (3 years ago in Galilee we protected the governor during village tour. Locals rioted, state guards fled, we subdued crowd, beat back rebels, returned Herod and retinue home.) **EXPERIENCE**

2 years ago—adjunct security for Cleopatra's birthday celebration in Alexandria. Did parade route security, temple security. Our undercover priest stuck with Cleopatra during sacrifices. On that job, pre-festival investigation uncovered rebellious cousin plotting assassination—dispatched her early with poisoned dagger made to simulate bite of an asp. **EXPERIENCE**

We train with South Britain's Belgic tribes—famous for fierceness and strategic excellence. **EXPERTISE**

We've got daggers, spears, bows, arrows, armor—all from top weaponsmiths in Rome. **EQUIPMENT**

We keep it quiet. No one in Alexandria knew we were protecting
Cleopatra. People still think her cousin died of snakebite (govern-
ment ruled it suicide). **DISCRETION**

We know what Caesar needs. Investigated soothsayer Spurrina's warn-
ing, Calpurnia's dreams, and the bad entrails. Based on evidence,
we'll focus on security from midmorning of the Ides through Senate
meeting. **CLIENT'S NEEDS**

Understand the need for secrecy. Senators might have conspired to
weaken centurion guard. So (as Caesar advised) we'd make his
friend Marcus Brutus security liaison. **CLIENT'S NEEDS**

We know the rules. Work ends at the Senate door. **EXPERTISE**

Our plan:

Coordinator: Marcus Valerius **PLAN**

Nones March through the Ides, our scouts interview associates and
potential rivals, check parade route, secure Senate area. **PLAN**

On the Ides:

Hire first-class fortune-teller to warn us of trouble. **PLAN**

Line parade route with plain-toga security, armed with concealed dag-
gers. **PLAN**

Station our own gladiators (in full armor) around the Forum.
PLAN

Station expert archers on the rooftop of the Forum buildings. **PLAN**

Employ fleet-footed runners to carry messages from the field to Marcus
Valerius (overseeing operation from command center in a corner
shop of the Forum). **PLAN**

Plan enables Caesar to be secure while showing strong face to masses.
He can publicly dismiss government guard and know we're on the
job. Except for Brutus, no one outside of Mercenary Security will
know of our involvement. **PLAN**

Breakdown of fees, based on hourly billing rates: **FEES**

Partner: 1 denarius

2 Scouts: 1 sestertii

1 fortune-teller: 1 sestertii

Gladiators: 1 dupondii

Message runners: 2 copper semisses

Plain-toga security: 1 quinarii

Archers: 3 sestertii

Personal bodyguards: 1 sestertii

Estimated time:

Partner and scouts—one week

Others—Ides, for three hours

Total estimate: 105 denarii (includes margin for out-of-pocket expenses)

We require half in advance.

Fee increases up to 20 percent if we see major combat or if more than one quarter of our men are killed. **FEES**

"Mercenary guarantee"—lead partner poisons himself if project fails. (Good track record—we're all still here.) **GUARANTEE**

Our motto: primo confuto, deinde caedo furtim, tandem eradico (*first suppress, then kill with stealth, finally crush*). **MOTTO**

Step 5: Choose Development 3—Point of Insight

Here are our categories:

EXPERIENCE

EXPERTISE

EQUIPMENT

DISCRETION

CLIENT'S NEEDS

PLAN

FEES

GUARANTEE

MOTTO

If our bottom line is that the combination of our skill, experience, and expertise makes us best for the job, what is the reader's Point of Insight? What comes just before that final sum-up?

Inexperienced proposal writers commonly make the mistake of leaving weaknesses for last. They believe that putting something last relegates it to the least important position in a piece of writing. Therefore, if price is our weakness, they'd make the case for our strengths and then slip in the price at the end, hoping the reader won't really notice it too much, after all that great stuff at the top. Wrong.

In writing, power comes at the end. Remember that we want the reader reading this way: Oh, good point. Oh! Even better! OH!! Yes! I'm sold! Put your weakness in Development 3, and this is the kind of Point of Insight your reader will have: Oh, good point. Oh! Even better. OH NO! I can't afford that! Forget it.

So if you're tempted to put our fees in the third Development, stifle the urge. As we're building this argument, we don't want to undercut ourselves just as we've won over the reader. What then does go in D3?

We have several strengths. We're strong on skill, experience, and the plan we're offering. How do we choose which of these ought to be the climactic point?

In this case it's got to be our detailed plan. It's wonderful that we've got skills and experience, but the reader needs to see how we'd put those to work for *him*. By the end of our proposal, we want Caesar visualizing the day of the Ides—and how confident he can be on his way to the Senate because Mercenary Security has thought of everything.

Our reader's Point of Insight, then, will be that our plan proves our expertise. Label all our "plan" notes D3, and fill in the outline:

You say:		The reader says:
Problem: Caesar needs expertise.		You're right. This is a complicated job. But how do I know you're the experts?
Development 1 (Background):		
Development 2 (Bridge):		
Development 3 (Point of Insight): Plan proves expertise.		Fantastic plan! I'd never have thought of all those details. You really are leagues ahead of the competition!
Resolution: We provide expertise.		You're hired!

Step 6: Choose Development 1—Background

EXPERIENCE

EXPERTISE

EQUIPMENT

DISCRETION

CLIENT'S NEEDS

PLAN **D3**

FEES

GUARANTEE

MOTTO

With our point of insight firmly in place, what background will help the reader begin to move toward our bottom line? In this case, the urge not to sabotage yourself up front with weaknesses is a correct one. Although when making an argument, you dispense with your opponent's point first, this doesn't apply when you've got a real weakness. In arguments, you have a response to the opposing viewpoint. In a proposal, where you have a serious weakness such as high price, there's no arguing it away. Therefore, don't put price as D1 simply to dispense with it before moving on to stronger points. Do that and you risk the reader putting down the proposal after the first page.

What *will* be Development 1? Reviewing our categories, you'll see we've got background material to spare. Our skills, our training and expertise, our discretion, and our previous experience are all background, as they tell the reader who we are and what we bring to the job. So what's the bottom line of our background chunk?

Choose this the same way you choose the bottom line for the whole piece of writing. The point that will most impress Caesar here is likely to be our previous work in very similar settings. Once he sees how we've protected his lover Cleopatra, he's much more likely to want us at the Forum on the Ides of March. The bottom line, then, will be our experience. Label it and slip it into the outline:

You say:	The reader says:
Problem: Caesar needs expertise.	*You're right. This is a complicated job. But how do I know you're the experts?*
Development 1 (Background): Experience shows expertise.	*Wow, Cleopatra—you guys must be good.*
Development 2 (Bridge):	
Development 3 (Point of Insight): Plan proves expertise.	*Fantastic plan! I'd never have thought of all those details. You really are leagues ahead of the competition!*
Resolution: We provide expertise.	*You're hired!*

Step 7: Choose Development 2—Bridge

EXPERIENCE **D1**

EXPERTISE **D1**

EQUIPMENT **D1**

DISCRETION **D1**

CLIENT'S NEEDS

PLAN **D3**

FEES

GUARANTEE

MOTTO

Although Development 2 often is the longest section of a piece of writing, that will not be the case here, because in this proposal, where we have a serious weakness to take on, we'll need to use the Bridge Development to do it. If your company's weakness is a small one, it could find its way into the List Outline, as one of many smaller details that need to be addressed on the way to the strong bottom line of a chunk of writing.

However, with a big weakness like price, which *must* be a large part of any proposal (the reader is, after all, inherently interested in how much this will cost him) you've got to spend one of your Developments on it. Cushioning it between two strong sections helps this a little. Moving the weakness closer to being a strength helps even more.

How do we make our high fees look good? We turn them into an investment. Everyone knows you get what you pay for, and if we talk about our fees in terms of the investment Caesar is making in a really quality service, he'll see the higher price in the context of paying top dollar (or denarius) to get the best. In addition, with a skillful breakdown of fees, we can show Caesar we've already thought through all his needs, a prelude to the fantastic plan we'll offer in D3. When, in our outline statement, we frame our fees in terms of an investment, we'll be reminded to write it that way, too.

You say:	The reader says:
Problem: Caesar needs expertise.	You're right. This is a complicated job. But how do I know you're the experts?
Development 1 (Background): Experience shows expertise.	Wow, Cleopatra—you guys must be good.
Development 2 (Bridge): Investment buys expertise.	You certainly have quite a breakdown of the people working on this project. It's costly, but it just might be worth it . . .
Development 3 (Point of Insight): Plan proves expertise.	Fantastic plan! I'd never have thought of all those details. You really are leagues ahead of the competition!
Resolution: We provide expertise.	You're hired!

Step 8: Create a List Outline—Organize Categories and Details

Problem: Caesar needs expertise.

Development 1: Experience shows expertise.

Development 2: Investment buys expertise.

Development 3: Plan proves expertise.

Resolution: We provide expertise.

```
┌────────────────────────────────────────────┐
│                                            │
└────────────────────────────────────────────┘
                      ▼
          **Problem: Caesar needs expertise.**


┌────────────────────────────────────────────┐
│              EXPERIENCE                     │
│              EQUIPMENT                      │
│              DISCRETION                     │
│              EXPERTISE                      │
└────────────────────────────────────────────┘
                      ▼
   **Development 1 (Background): Experience shows expertise.**


┌────────────────────────────────────────────┐
│                  FEES                      │
└────────────────────────────────────────────┘
                      ▼
    **Development 2 (Bridge): Investment buys expertise.**


┌────────────────────────────────────────────┐
│                  PLAN                      │
└────────────────────────────────────────────┘
                      ▼
  **Development 3 (Point of Insight): Plan proves expertise.**


┌────────────────────────────────────────────┐
│                                            │
└────────────────────────────────────────────┘
                      ▼
          **Resolution: We provide expertise.**
```

Notes: The Background Development here needs reorganizing. As experience is our bottom line there, it should come last. Work backward from there. Discretion goes directly to our experience—we dispatched Cleopatra's cousin without anyone knowing—so that comes second to last. How well equipped we are only matters if we know how to use those weapons—based on our training. Therefore, put expertise first, then equipment, then discretion, then experience.

The categories of guarantee, client's needs, and our company's motto so far don't have a place. Client's needs clearly belong in the Problem. If we don't understand his needs, we don't go anywhere. But guarantee could go with experience, or it could end up in the Resolution, as a parting gift to Caesar. This is a judgment call. Let's put it in the Resolution, because it leaves the reader with a sense of our style—we put our money where our mouth is. As far as our motto, that might work well in our experience section, because our experience in Alexandria and Galilee shows us living that motto (killing Cleopatra's cousin with poison, subduing villagers in battle).

Now our outline looks like this:

> CLIENT'S NEEDS

Problem: Caesar needs expertise.

> EXPERTISE
> EQUIPMENT
> DISCRETION
> EXPERIENCE
> MOTTO

Development 1 (Background): Experience shows expertise.

> FEES

Development 2 (Bridge): Investment buys expertise.

PLAN

Development 3 (Point of Insight): Plan proves expertise.

GUARANTEE

Resolution: We provide expertise.

Time to shift from categories to notes, though we'll keep the categories, too, to help us continue to organize our more complicated piece:

Problem: Caesar needs expertise

Development 1: Experience shows expertise.

Development 2: Investment buys expertise.

Development 3: Plan proves expertise.

Resolution: We provide expertise.

> *We know what Caesar needs. Investigated soothsayer Spurrina's warning, Calpurnia's*
> *dreams, and the bad entrails. Based on evidence, we'll focus on security from mid-*
> *morning of the Ides through Senate meeting.* **CLIENT'S NEEDS**
> *Understand the need for secrecy. Senators might have conspired to weaken centurion*
> *guard. So (as Caesar advised) we'd make his friend Marcus Brutus security liaison.*
> **CLIENT'S NEEDS**

Problem: Caesar needs expertise.

We train with South Britain's Belgic tribes—famous for fierceness and strategic excellence. **EXPERTISE**

We know the rules. Work ends at the Senate door. **EXPERTISE**

We've got daggers, spears, bows, arrows, armor—all from top weapon-smiths in Rome. **EQUIPMENT**

We keep it quiet. No one in Alexandria knew we were protecting Cleopatra. People still think her cousin died of snakebite (government ruled it suicide). **DISCRETION**

Heads of state our specialty for 25 years. (We've protected Herod, Cleopatra.) **EXPERIENCE**

Herod (3 years ago in Galilee we protected the governor during village tour. Locals rioted, state guards fled, we subdued crowd, beat back rebels, returned Herod and retinue home.) **EXPERIENCE**

2 years ago—adjunct security for Cleopatra's birthday celebration in Alexandria. Did parade route security, temple security. Our undercover priest stuck with Cleopatra during sacrifices. On that job, pre-festival investigation uncovered rebellious cousin plotting assassination—dispatched her early with poisoned dagger made to simulate bite of an asp. **EXPERIENCE**

Our motto: primo confuto, deinde caedo furtim, tandem eradico (first suppress, then kill with stealth, finally crush). **MOTTO**

Development 1 (Background): Experience shows expertise.

Breakdown of fees, based on hourly billing rates: **FEES**

Partner: 1 denarius

2 Scouts: 1 sestertii

1 fortune-teller: 1 sestertii

Gladiators: 1 dupondii

Message runners: 2 copper semisses

Plain-toga security: 1 quinarii

Archers: 3 sestertii

Personal bodyguards: 1 sestertii

Estimated time:

Partner and scouts—one week

Others—Ides, for three hours

Total estimate: 105 denarii (includes margin for out-of-pocket expenses)

We require half in advance.

Fee increases up to 20 percent if we see major combat or if more than one quarter of our men are killed. **FEES**

Development 2 (Bridge): Investment buys expertise.

Our plan:

Coordinator: Marcus Valerius **PLAN**

Nones March through the Ides, our scouts interview associates and potential rivals, check parade route, secure Senate area. **PLAN**

On the Ides:

Hire first-class fortune-teller to warn us of trouble. **PLAN**

Line parade route with plain-toga security, armed with concealed daggers. **PLAN**

Station our own gladiators (in full armor) around the Forum. **PLAN**

Station expert archers on the rooftop of the Forum buildings. **PLAN**

Employ fleet-footed runners to carry messages from the field to Marcus Valerius (overseeing operation from command center in a corner shop of the Forum). **PLAN**

Plan enables Caesar to be secure while showing strong face to masses. He can publicly dismiss government guard and know we're on the job. Except for Brutus, no one outside of Mercenary Security will know of our involvement. **PLAN**

Development 3 (Point of Insight): Plan proves expertise.

> *"Mercenary guarantee"—lead partner poisons himself if project fails. (Good track record—we're all still here.)* **GUARANTEE**

Resolution: We provide expertise.

Notice that when we evaluate our actual notes, we have some further work to do in organizing specifics. When reviewing your note-filled List Outline, always ask yourself:

- Does the logic hold together? Does each point lead smoothly to the next?
- Do all the points drive toward the bottom line of that chunk?
- Is anything missing?

Reviewing this List Outline, we can see the following:

1. In the "Client's needs" section in our Problem, the specific discussion of how we will maintain our discretion on this job is too detailed for the opening section. We do need to mention that we'll be discreet, but we need to save the specifics for Development 3—the plan. Therefore, leave a general note on discretion in the Problem and move the specifics down.

2. We have a similar problem in Development 1, where we discuss our expertise specifically in reference to knowing the rules of the Roman Senate. Although this is part of our expert knowledge, it has more to do with the job in Rome than with any of our previous experience. Therefore, remove it from its place in D1 and put it down as part of the discussion of our plan, in Development 3.

3. With the misplaced note removed, it's clear D1 needs further organization. At the moment, we move from the idea of our training and weaponry to a note about our discretion. Since discretion relates to the Alexandria

job, that must come first, then we can move to our protection of Herod, where we had to resort to fighting a full battle in the street against angry rebels. Our motto might fit well as the introduction to the example of our discretion in Alexandria. Put it there.

This kind of shifting around is typical once you begin to write complex pieces. Broad categories take you halfway—they get most of your notes in the right chunk of your outline. But they can only take you so far. Once you move down to the details, you must reevaluate yet again. With most of the notes in the right place, it's easier to spot pieces that don't belong and reorganize them to group information that makes the same point, for example, that we're discreet. In the List Outline, you're even able to smooth out the flow on the sentence level, so that you shift naturally from List Outline to draft.

Each time you move forward with the outline—from Target to List and from categories of notes to actual notes—you have another chance to evaluate your ideas. This is one big benefit of the Target Outline System: You can organize language and information as you go, so the task never becomes overwhelming.

After evaluating what you already have, turn your attention to what's missing:

1. The Problem chunk doesn't yet offer an overview of the proposal—a sentence to tell the reader what's coming. It also does not quite make the point that what Caesar needs most is expert help. Write sentences that do both these jobs, and move the rest of your notes closer to full sentences.

2. The Resolution is nearly empty. Our guarantee is fine, but only as part of a larger point that we have what Caesar needs. The Resolution here requires a sum-up of all the facts in our favor—and a revisiting of the theme of expertise as it applies to everything we've told Caesar. In addition, the proposal needs a closing sentence that identifies the next step we hope Caesar will take—getting in touch with us to seal the deal.

3. The Bridge Development (D2) does not yet make the point that paying our fees can be seen as an investment in real expertise. Write a sentence to that effect to end the Development.

Before we move on to transitions and the opening hook, look at the outline with these further refinements, to see how far we've come (new additions are in bold):

Problem: Caesar needs expertise.

Development 1: Experience shows expertise.

Development 2: Investment buys expertise.

Development 3: Plan proves expertise.

Resolution: We provide expertise.

> *We understand your requirements. We pay attention to all portents, symbols, and signs. As such, we have duly noted and scrutinized the soothsayer Spurrina's warning to beware the Ides of March, as well as your wife Calpurnia's dreams and the bad omens found in the entrails of your recent sacrifices. Given the evidence, we have focused our attention on protection for midmorning of the Ides, through your Senate meeting that day.*
>
> ***This proposal sets out our understanding of your needs, the experience we bring to bear on them, an estimate of the fees for our services, and our approach to your project. [introductory sentence]***
>
> *We are also aware of the need for absolute secrecy in our preparations. Discretion has been the Mercenary standard for all its years in business, and we would maintain the highest level of secrecy when providing security on the Ides.*
>
> ***Safeguarding a head of state requires more than bodyguards and soldiers. With a quarter century of experience in the field of leader-protection, we at Mercenary know well the expertise such a job requires and are pleased to present our plan for protecting you on that important day. [sentence to draw the reader to the point of the Problem]***

Problem: Caesar needs expertise.

Our men train among the Belgic tribes in Southern Britain, a people known for their fierceness and their strategic excellence.

We are well equipped. Our weapons—from daggers to spears to bows and arrows and armor—are of the highest quality and come from the top weapon-smiths in Rome.

We are discreet. The Mercenary motto is: primo confuto, deinde caedo furtim, tandem eradico (first suppress, then kill with stealth, finally crush).

Two years ago, we served as adjunct security for Cleopatra in Alexandria, on the occasion of her public birthday celebration. When our pre-festival investigation uncovered a rebellious cousin plotting to assassinate the queen, we dispatched her before the festival with a poisoned dagger specially designed to mimic the bite of an asp. Our work in Egypt included parade route security, as well as temple security, in which we sent in undercover priests to remain close to Cleopatra during sacrifices.

No one in Egypt knew that we had been hired to protect the queen, and, as the festivities proceeded without incident, our participation remains unknown. Because of our discretion in poisoning Cleopatra's cousin, a government investigation ruled her death a suicide.

Three years ago, in Galilee, we protected Governor Herod during his tour of the villagers. When the locals rioted and Herod's state guards fled, we subdued the crowd, beat back the rebels, and returned Herod safely to his residence, along with his retinue.

Development 1 (Background): Experience shows expertise.

Breakdown of our fees, based on the following hourly billing rates:

Partner: 1 denarius

2 Scouts: 1 sestertii

1 fortune-teller: 1 sestertii

Gladiators: 1 dupondii

Message runners: 2 copper semisses

Plain-toga security: 1 quinarii

Archers: 3 sestertii

Personal bodyguards: 1 sestertii

We estimate that the partner and scouts will work for a week on this project, and the other personnel will work only on the Ides, for three hours—from the time you leave home through your meeting at the Senate. Therefore, we estimate the fee for our full-service security at 105 denarii, which includes a small margin for out-of-pocket expenses. Of this, we require half in advance. This fee will increase by up to 20 percent if our personnel see major combat or if more than one quarter of them are killed.

Our extensive planning and expert personnel keep out-of-pocket expenses to a minimum. At Mercenary, we prepare for all reasonable contingencies to avoid cost overruns while keeping you secure.

Development 2 (Bridge): Investment buys expertise.

We have a detailed plan:

Marcus Valerius, a senior partner in Mercenaries Security would coordinate this very important job.

We would send scouts out from the Nones of March until the Ides, to interview associates and potential rivals, to check the parade route, and secure the area of the Senate.

We would employ a first-class fortune-teller on the day of the Ides, to alert us of any negative developments.

On the Ides, we would line the parade route with plain-toga security, who, armed with concealed daggers, would be ready for any attacks.

We would station gladiators of our own, in full armor, around the Forum.

We would have expert archers on the rooftop of the Forum buildings, to watch as you enter the Senate.

We would employ several fleet-footed runners to carry messages from the field to Marcus Valerius, who would oversee the operation during the Ides from our command center in a corner shop of the Forum.

This plan would enable you to maintain security while radiating confidence to the masses. You will be able to publicly dismiss your government bodyguard, while knowing we remain on the job. With the exception of your trusted ally Brutus, no one outside of Mercenary Security will know of our involvement.

Development 3 (Point of Insight): Plan proves expertise.

In summary, we believe Mercenary Security is uniquely qualified to protect you on the Ides of March. Our experience working with other heads of state under similar circumstances, our extensive and highly trained personnel, and the expertise that we bring to planning this engagement will be invaluable to this effort. [sum-up sentence]

As always, we include our "Mercenary guarantee"—the lead partner poisons himself if the project fails. Our track record of success is excellent, however—we are all still alive.

We are anxious to work with you and hope that we can discuss this proposal in more detail in the coming week. If you have any questions, please contact us by courier. [sentence that identifies the action we hope the client will take]

Resolution: We provide expertise.

Step 9: Add Transitions and an Opening Hook

Basic transitions in this proposal will move the reader through time ("Three years ago . . .") and from subject to subject ("We understand that you require . . . ," "In summary . . ."). They smooth the way for the reader as he moves from one section to the next. Instead of the abrupt "We have a detailed plan" of our notes (the opening of our D3), a smooth transition would read: "Based on our understanding of your needs and the challenges involved [a reference back to the previous sections], we have prepared a preliminary plan to protect you on the Ides of March."

However, transitions in this proposal can also take on an additional role. They can—and should—keep the theme of the proposal alive from section to section.

At the opening of each new chunk of the outline, transitions not only serve as mini introductions, connecting the subject we've just discussed to the subject we're introducing, but they can show the reader how our proposal's theme relates to the upcoming subject.

For example, in the opening of our experience section (D1), we currently jump right into the facts—our training among the Belgic tribes. With a moment of transition, we could remind the reader that our training is what makes us so qualified. Use a sentence like "Mercenary Security's experience makes us uniquely qualified for this engagement."

Again, in the opening of D2, where we introduce our fees, our outline now moves directly to a list of hourly rates. Better by far to open with a sentence or two to cushion the prices and remind Caesar why we're worth it: "Mercenary's pricing structure takes into account all aspects of your project, including the personnel, equipment, and man-hours required to make it a success. Given the scope of your engagement and the personnel involved, our fees for this project would be based on the hourly billing rates shown below:"

THE OPENING HOOK

In an informal proposal, the opening hook will generally address the reader directly and refer to any previous contact the writer has had with the potential client. Dispense with the abrupt "We understand your needs" of our notes and write: "Dear Caesar, It was a pleasure meeting with you to discuss your security needs for the Ides of March." Then launch directly into the theme: "At Mercenary Security, we recognize the importance of protecting the ruler of the known world. Therefore, we pay attention to all portents . . ."

Step 10: Polish Your Draft

Your draft is almost complete already. To polish it, go over your language one more time, to make sure the sentences flow. Insert white space, headings, and bulleted lists to make the proposal easy on the eye, and sign your name at the end. Now take a look at the document you're sending Caesar (Target Outline elements included in capitals and List Outline elements in bold and in parentheses):

To Julius Caesar, Dictator Perpetuo

(opening hook)

Dear Caesar,

It was a pleasure meeting with you to discuss your security needs for the Ides of March. At Mercenary Security, we recognize the importance of protecting the ruler of the known world **(end of opening hook)**. Therefore, **(transition)** we pay attention to all portents, symbols, and signs. The signs you mentioned— the soothsayer Spurrina's warning to beware the Ides, your wife Calpurnia's dreams, and the bad omens found in the entrails of your recent sacrifices— provide more than adequate warning that you need protection on your way to the Senate this March. Given the evidence, we have focused our attention on protection for midmorning of the Ides through your Senate meeting. This proposal sets out our understanding of your needs, the experience we can bring to bear on them, an estimate of the fees for our services, and our approach to your project.

Our Understanding of Your Needs (transition)

We understand that you require full-service security from your departure from home on the morning of the Ides of March through your meeting with the senators. We also understand the need for absolute secrecy in our preparations and execution of this task. Discretion has been the Mercenary standard for 25 years, and we would maintain the highest level of secrecy when providing security on the Ides.

Safeguarding a head of state requires more than bodyguards and soldiers. With a quarter century of experience in the field of leader-protection, we at Mercenary know well the expertise such a job requires and are pleased to present our plan for protecting you on that important day.

PROBLEM: CAESAR NEEDS EXPERTISE.

Our Experience (transition)

Mercenary Security's experience makes us uniquely qualified for this engagement **(transition)**. Our men train among the Belgic tribes in Southern Britain, a people known for their strategic brilliance and their excellence in battle. We arm these highly trained personnel with the latest in weaponry. All our daggers, spears, bows, arrows, and armor come from the top weapon-smiths in Rome.

Armed and ready for battle, **(transition)** we also practice great discretion, avoiding confrontation where possible. The Mercenary motto is *primo confuto, deinde caedo furtim, tandem eradico* (first suppress, then kill with stealth, finally crush). Two years ago, we served as adjunct security for Cleopatra in Alexandria, on the occasion of her public birthday celebration. When our pre-festival investigation uncovered a rebellious cousin plotting to assassinate the queen, we dispatched her before the festival with a poisoned dagger specially designed to mimic the bite of an asp. Our work in Egypt included parade route and temple security, in which we sent undercover priests to remain close to Cleopatra during sacrifices. Our forces kept order so silently most Egyptians did not know of our involvement, and a government investigation into the death of Cleopatra's cousin ruled it a suicide.

Though discretion is our watchword, **(transition)** we can and will do battle when necessary. Three years ago, in Galilee, we protected Governor Herod during his tour of the villagers. When the locals rioted and Herod's state guards fled, we subdued the crowd, beat back the rebels, and returned Herod safely to his residence, along with his retinue.

DEVELOPMENT 1: EXPERIENCE SHOWS EXPERTISE.

Professional Fees **(transition)**

Mercenary's pricing structure takes into account all aspects of your project, including the personnel, equipment, and man-hours required to make it a success **(transition)**. Given the scope of your engagement and the personnel involved, our fees for this project would be based on the hourly billing rates shown below:

Partner: 1 denarius

Scouts: 1 sestertii

Fortune-teller: 1 sestertii

Gladiators: 1 dupondii

Message runners: 2 copper semisses

Plain-toga security: 1 quinarii

Archers: 3 sestertii

Personal bodyguards: 1 sestertii

We estimate that the partner and scouts would work for a week on this project, and the other personnel would work only on the Ides, for three hours—from the time you leave home through your Senate meeting. Therefore, we estimate the fee for our full-service security at 105 denarii, which includes a small margin for out-of-pocket expenses. Of this, we require half in advance. This fee will increase by up to 20 percent if our personnel see major combat or if more than one quarter of them are killed.

Our extensive planning and expert personnel keep out-of-pocket expenses to a minimum. With Mercenary, we prepare for all reasonable contingencies to avoid cost overruns while keeping you secure.

DEVELOPMENT 2: INVESTMENT BUYS EXPERTISE.

Our Approach to This Engagement

Based on our understanding of your needs and the challenges involved, we have prepared a preliminary plan to protect you on the Ides of March **(transition)**. Mercenary would:

• Provide a senior partner, Marcus Valerius, to coordinate all Ides-related security.

• Send scouts out from the Nones of March until the Ides, to interview associates and potential rivals, to check the parade route, and to secure the area of the Senate.

• Employ a certified fortune-teller on the day of the Ides, to alert us of any negative developments.

• Line the parade route with plain-toga security, who, armed with concealed daggers, would be ready for any attacks.

• Station gladiators of our own, in full armor, around the Forum.

• Station archers on the rooftop of the Forum buildings, to watch as you enter the Senate.

• Employ several fleet-footed runners to carry messages from the field to Marcus Valerius, who would oversee the operation during the Ides from our command center in a corner shop of the Forum.

This plan would enable you to maintain security while radiating confidence to the masses. You would be able to publicly dismiss your government bodyguard, while knowing we remain on the job. With the exception of your trusted ally Marcus Brutus, with whom you suggested we coordinate, no one outside of Mercenary Security will know of our involvement.

DEVELOPMENT 3: PLAN PROVES EXPERTISE.

In summary, **(transition)** we believe Mercenary Security is uniquely qualified to protect you on the Ides of March. Our experience working with other heads of state under similar circumstances, our extensive and highly trained personnel, and the expertise that we bring to planning this engagement will be invaluable to this effort. As always, we offer the Mercenary guarantee: if we fail, the partner in charge of the engagement drinks poison. You can rest assured we have an excellent success rate as, to date, we all remain alive.

We are anxious to work with you and hope that we can discuss this proposal in more detail in the coming week. If you have any questions, please contact us by courier.

Very truly yours,

Marcus Valerius, Cyriacus Aggripa, and Cato Octavius

Partners, Mercenary Security

RESOLUTION: WE PROVIDE EXPERTISE.

A NOTE ON WRITING FORMAL PROPOSALS

When large companies or the government put out a Request for Proposal (RFP), they usually dictate the exact structure of the document they want in response. Although you might lack experience, or have a higher-than-average price, you have no choice but to detail that information where they want it. How do you handle this?

In the case of such formal proposals, the answer is to use transitions. Just as in an informal proposal, assess your strengths and weaknesses. Develop a theme that highlights those strengths and transforms, or at least cushions, the weaknesses. Then write transitions into each section that put experience, or fees, or whatever the section requires, in terms of your theme. If you've decided to stress that you make up for your company's relative lack of experience by being innovative and fresh, bring that in when you introduce the experience section. Allude to it again when you tout your lower-than-average fees. Although you don't have control over the structure of the overall document, if you create a Target Outline that highlights your theme, you'll still have control of your message.

Another way to use transitions in this context is to be aware that many words convey not only information, but connotation. You can use such words to create **melding transitions**—transitions that marry two ideas. If your fees are high, but you want to convey that the reader will be getting a quality product for that price, you might use the word "investment," which conveys the idea of money well spent. For example: "An investment in Technology Incorporated means on-time delivery of a flawless product." Using melding words in your transitions in a formal proposal can help convey your theme even when you're forced to follow a prescribed structure.

CHAPTER 9

MARKETING PROPOSALS

Marketing proposals stand out from other proposals because they sell *ideas*, not products or services. Like research proposals—which solicit funds for scientific or technical studies—marketing proposals attempt to show the reader that an idea is worth pursuing with time and money. Of all the forms of persuasive writing required in business, marketing proposals call for the most creativity. Therefore, in this chapter, you'll learn how to use innovative openings and complex transitions—tools that do more than simply order your work in a logical sequence. Here you'll learn not just how to draw the reader in and guide him through, but how to grab him and set him on an adventure.

Intent: The intent of a marketing proposal is to:

- Explore the current market or research on a subject
- Introduce the reader to your new idea/product/service
- Identify the market for that product or service
- Show why the product or service will succeed

Bottom Line: The bottom line of a marketing proposal is to:

- Convince the reader to fund or pursue an idea or project

The System in 10 Easy Steps

You work for the research and development department of a medium-sized beverage company, Get Me a Drink, Inc. The company sells bottled water, but its president wants to expand into a new area of the market. She's asked you to come up with ideas.

Step 1: Questions and Research

1. **Who is my audience?** Bubbles McGee, President, Get Me a Drink, Inc.
2. **What does she want to know?** What new product will help her company grow?
3. **What is my bottom line point?** (see below)

Find out:

- What beverage market is both fast-growing and still open to new entries
- What product could help the company break into that market
- The market's history
- The market's profitability
- What the current market looks like
- Which consumers you would target
- How you would market your new product

Step 2: Evaluate Your Notes and Determine the Bottom Line

Unlike our earlier examples, this proposal calls for both research and creative thought. Imagine that you studied the current beverage market and discovered that while sodas and bottled fruit drinks already saturate the market, the field of energy drinks, while popular, still leaves room for newcomers. You'd then go research that market. Here are your notes:

Early energy drinks: Jolt, Red Bull.

Red Bull is market leader—has 60 percent market share.

Last year energy drinks sold $1.1 billion in U.S. market.

Jolt, created 1985, was soda with more caffeine.

Red Bull, created 1987, took Japanese energy drinks and marketed them to Western consumers.

Red Bull active ingredients—taurine and vitamins added to caffeine and other ingredients.

Energy drinks sell for $2 for an 8-ounce can.

Market has grown 700 percent in the last five years; still growing.

Success attributed to marketing.

Young men are target market.

Market also targets hip hop fans and video game users.

Energy drink companies usually sponsor extreme sports events to attract consumers.

Red Bull sponsorships:

paraglider across the Grand Canyon

homemade aircraft flying

Go Fast! plans to sponsor a skydiver in a wing suit; no parachute.

Other marketing sponsorships by drink-makers: snowboarding, bridge jumping, rocket launches.

Pepsi and Coke introduced energy drinks this year to the same sports-oriented market.

Energy drinks are mildly carbonated.

Consumers complain about medicine-like taste.

Energy drink market can still grow. Today it's only 2 percent of the $60 billion soft drink market.

From preliminary research, you've been able to get a picture, so far, of the current energy drink market. It's big, and expected to keep growing. It targets young men, and mostly does it with nontraditional marketing techniques—sponsoring extreme sports events to get fans' attention.

If you simply needed to write a report on the energy drink market, you'd have nearly enough here. But your company wants more. It's looking to expand into that market. From the research you've already done, you can see that won't work if you just create another Red Bull clone. Pepsi and Coke are both entering that market with sports-oriented drinks, and a small company like yours won't stand a chance.

You do a little thinking, and realize that there is an unserved market here—it's filled with women and men who want energy, but not for extreme sports.

Imagine you thought about that for a while and decided to direct your product to what you might call the genius demographic—people who want extra energy for creative tasks, like science, art, music, and computer design. You call your new product Brainstorm and jot down the following ideas:

> *"Geniuses" need energy to stay up late, studying and creating.*
> *Who are they? Teens and adults, men and women in science, engineering, computers, art, music, dance.*
> *Add extra dose of pyridoxine (B_6), said to boost creativity, as our special ingredient.*
> *Brainstorm could be marketed in a lightbulb-shaped can, to highlight its "genius" focus.*
> *Marketing ideas:*
> *Taste tests with memory tests*
> *Computer game tournaments*
> *Alternative music festivals*
> *Campus art/music/poetry promotions*

Engineering design contests

"Can you get in?" marketing idea—consumers take IQ tests to prove
    they can "drink the drink."

Brainstorm tagline: "Carbonate your inner genius."

Brainstorm could come in both sugar and sugar-free versions. It would
    be highly carbonated to "pop" with creativity.

Next step: analyze startup costs for this project.

Possibly sell Brainstorm for slightly less than other energy drinks (use
    smaller bottles like soda makers do) and gain advantage that way.

The bottom line? Now we're approaching something like a bottom line. Look again at all your notes. Clearly, your bottom line is something like: "Brainstorm will get our company into the energy market. It has the potential for success, because it serves a different kind of consumer." That moves the reader from her need—to expand the business—to your particular response to that need: Brainstorm.

Step 3: Identify the Problem and Resolution

You say:

Problem: A new product, Brainstorm, could offer Get Me a Drink, Inc., a way into the lucrative energy drink market.

Resolution: Brainstorm will succeed because it serves a different kind of consumer.

The reader says:

Well, I am interested in expanding. How will Brainstorm help me do it?

Oh! That's how! Give this genius a promotion!

Step 4: Categorize Your Notes

Early energy drinks: Jolt, Red Bull. **HISTORY OF THE MARKET**

Red Bull is market leader—has 60 percent market share. **THE MAR-KET TODAY**

Last year energy drinks sold $1.1 billion in U.S. market. **THE MAR-KET TODAY**

Jolt, created 1985, was soda with more caffeine. **HISTORY OF THE MARKET**

Red Bull, created 1987, took Japanese energy drinks and marketed them to Western consumers. **HISTORY OF THE MARKET**

Red Bull active ingredients—taurine and vitamins added to caffeine and other ingredients. **WHAT ARE ENERGY DRINKS?**

Energy drinks sell for $2 for an 8-ounce can. **WHAT ARE ENERGY DRINKS?**

Market has grown 700 percent in the last five years; still growing. **THE MARKET TODAY**

Success attributed to marketing. **REASON FOR PRODUCT SUCCESS**

Young men are target market. **CURRENT TARGET MARKET**

Market also targets hip hop fans and video game users. **CURRENT TARGET MARKET**

Energy drink companies usually sponsor extreme sports events to attract consumers. **MARKETING IN CURRENT MARKET**

Red Bull sponsorships: **MARKETING IN CURRENT MARKET**

paraglider across the Grand Canyon **MARKETING IN CURRENT MARKET**

homemade aircraft flying **MARKETING IN CURRENT MARKET**

Go Fast! plans to sponsor a skydiver in wing suit; no parachute. **MAR-KETING IN CURRENT MARKET**

Other marketing sponsorships by drink-makers: snowboarding, bridge jumping, rocket launches. **MARKETING IN CURRENT MARKET**

Pepsi and Coke introduced energy drinks this year to same sports-oriented market. **THE MARKET TODAY**

Energy drinks are mildly carbonated. **WHAT ARE ENERGY DRINKS?**

Consumers complain about medicine-like taste. **PROBLEMS WITH THE PRODUCT**

Energy drink market can still grow. Today it's only 2 percent of the $60 billion soft drink market. **THE MARKET TODAY**

"Geniuses" need energy to stay up late, studying and creating. **UN-SERVED CONSUMERS**

Who are they? Teens and adults, men and women in science, engineering, computers, art, music, dance. **UNSERVED CONSUMERS**

Add extra dose of pyridoxine (B_6), said to boost creativity, as our special ingredient. **THE BRAINSTORM PRODUCT**

Brainstorm could be marketed in a lightbulb-shaped can, to highlight its "genius" focus. **THE BRAINSTORM PRODUCT**

Marketing ideas:

Taste tests with memory tests **HOW TO REACH THE BRAINSTORM CONSUMER**

Computer game tournaments **HOW TO REACH THE BRAINSTORM CONSUMER**

Alternative music festivals **HOW TO REACH THE BRAINSTORM CONSUMER**

Campus art/music/poetry promotions **HOW TO REACH THE BRAIN-STORM CONSUMER**

Engineering design contests **HOW TO REACH THE BRAINSTORM CONSUMER**

"Can you get in?" marketing idea—consumers take IQ tests to prove they can "drink the drink." **HOW TO REACH THE BRAINSTORM CONSUMER**

Brainstorm tagline: "Carbonate your inner genius." **HOW TO REACH THE BRAINSTORM CONSUMER**

Brainstorm could come in both sugar and sugar-free versions. It would be highly carbonated to "pop" with creativity. **THE BRAINSTORM PRODUCT**

Next step: analyze startup costs for this project. **NEXT STEP**

Possibly sell Brainstorm for slightly less than other energy drinks (use smaller bottles like soda makers do) and gain advantage that way. **THE BRAINSTORM PRODUCT**

Step 5: Choose Development 3—Point of Insight

Here are your categories:

HISTORY OF THE MARKET

THE MARKET TODAY

WHAT ARE ENERGY DRINKS?

REASON FOR PRODUCT SUCCESS

CURRENT TARGET MARKET

MARKETING IN CURRENT MARKET

PROBLEMS WITH THE PRODUCT

UNSERVED CONSUMERS

THE BRAINSTORM PRODUCT

HOW TO REACH THE BRAINSTORM CONSUMER

NEXT STEP

Which categories are most likely to get the company president to realize that Brainstorm has a real chance to succeed and help the company grow?

First the product itself—THE BRAINSTORM PRODUCT—and second, how that product would be marketed—HOW TO REACH THE BRAIN-

STORM CONSUMER. Once Bubbles McGee sees there are ways to reach a population that would drink Brainstorm but isn't being served by it, she'll realize this idea could help her company expand. Since the marketing plan—even more than the new product—shows how Brainstorm would become a success, the bottom line of your third Development will be something like: Marketing plan shows how Brainstorm could succeed.

You say:

Problem: A new product, Brainstorm, could offer Get Me a Drink, Inc., a way into the lucrative energy drink market.

Development 1 (Background)

Development 2 (Bridge)

Development 3 (Point of Insight): The marketing plan shows that Brainstorm has a good chance of success.

Resolution: Brainstorm will succeed because it serves a different kind of consumer.

The reader says:

Well, I am interested in expanding. How will this Brainstorm stuff help me do it?

It really does! Great idea!

Wow! Give this genius a promotion!

Once the company president sees *how* the product could reach those consumers, she can easily make the jump to the Resolution that Brainstorm *will* succeed.

Step 6: Choose Development 1—Background

HISTORY OF THE MARKET

THE MARKET TODAY

WHAT ARE ENERGY DRINKS?

REASON FOR PRODUCT SUCCESS

CURRENT TARGET MARKET

MARKETING IN CURRENT MARKET

PROBLEMS WITH THE PRODUCT

UNSERVED CONSUMERS

THE BRAINSTORM PRODUCT **D3**

HOW TO REACH THE BRAINSTORM CONSUMER **D3**

NEXT STEP

What background must the reader understand in order to launch her into this topic?

Obviously, she has to know what energy drinks are, who currently dominates the market, and whether the market can still grow. That would include our categories HISTORY OF THE MARKET, THE MARKET TODAY, WHAT ARE ENERGY DRINKS?, REASON FOR PRODUCT SUCCESS, and possibly PROBLEMS WITH THE PRODUCT. The bottom line of Development 1, however, would focus on the reader's area of interest—how to create a hit product. Therefore, the bottom line of D1 would use these categories to make that point: The energy drink market bursts with potential.

You say:	The reader says:
Problem: A new product, Brainstorm, could offer Get Me a Drink, Inc., a way into the lucrative energy drink market.	Well, I am interested in expanding. How will this Brainstorm stuff help me do it?
Development 1 (Background): The energy drink market bursts with potential.	Looks like a good place to try to expand. But how would we do it?
Development 2 (Bridge):	

Development 3 (Point of
    Insight): The marketing plan
    shows that Brainstorm has a
    good chance of success.
Resolution: Brainstorm will
    succeed because it serves a
    different kind of consumer.

It really does!

Great idea!

Wow! Give this

genius a promotion!

Step 7: Choose Development 2—Bridge

HISTORY OF THE MARKET **D1**

THE MARKET TODAY **D1**

WHAT ARE ENERGY DRINKS? **D1**

REASON FOR PRODUCT SUCCESS **D1**

CURRENT TARGET MARKET

MARKETING IN CURRENT MARKET

PROBLEMS WITH THE PRODUCT **D1**

UNSERVED CONSUMERS

THE BRAINSTORM PRODUCT **D3**

HOW TO REACH THE BRAINSTORM CONSUMER **D3**

NEXT STEP

Finally, what piece of logic is missing?

You've shown your reader that the energy drink market offers potential for growth. You've offered a plan for targeting an unserved consumer with a new product. What must connect the two? The unserved consumers you plan to go after. Who are they? You'll need not only to identify them, but to show how they differ from the current target market. Therefore, label as D2 your categories CURRENT TARGET MARKET, MARKETING IN THE CURRENT MARKET, and UNSERVED CONSUMERS.

To complete the Target Outline, fill in a Development 2 statement that addresses the unserved market out there that gives Brainstorm so much potential:

You say:	The reader says:
Problem: A new product, Brainstorm, could offer Get Me a Drink, Inc., a way into the lucrative energy drink market.	Well, I am interested in expanding. How will this Brainstorm stuff help me do it?
Development 1 (Background): The energy drink market bursts with potential.	Looks like a good place to try to expand. But how would we do it?
Development 2 (Bridge): The ignored "genius" consumer gives us a way to succeed in this market.	I can see that. Good point! How do we exploit this hole in the market?
Development 3 (Point of insight): The marketing plan shows that Brainstorm has a good chance of success.	That's how! We really can succeed. Great idea!
Resolution: Brainstorm will succeed because it serves a different kind of consumer.	Wow! Give this genius a promotion!

Step 8: Create a List Outline—Organize Categories and Details

Problem: Brainstorm offers growth.

Development 1 (Background): Market bursts with potential.

Development 2 (Bridge): Geniuses create a market.

Development 3 (Point of Insight): Plan shows how we'll succeed.

Resolution: Brainstorm will succeed because it serves a different kind of consumer.

> [blank box]

Problem: Brainstorm offers growth.

> HISTORY OF THE MARKET
> THE MARKET TODAY
> WHAT ARE ENERGY DRINKS?
> REASON FOR PRODUCT SUCCESS
> PROBLEMS WITH THE PRODUCT

Development 1 (Background): Market bursts with potential.

> CURRENT TARGET MARKET
> MARKETING IN CURRENT MARKET
> UNSERVED CONSUMERS

Development 2 (Bridge): Geniuses create market.

> THE BRAINSTORM PRODUCT
> HOW TO REACH THE BRAINSTORM CONSUMER

Development 3 (Point of Insight): Plan shows how we'll succeed.

> [blank box]

Resolution: Brainstorm will succeed because it serves a different kind of consumer.

Notes: Before we deal with the empty places and unlabeled spaces, let's organize the ideas we've already placed. At the moment, Development 1 holds five categories:

HISTORY OF THE MARKET

THE MARKET TODAY

WHAT ARE ENERGY DRINKS?

REASONS FOR PRODUCT SUCCESS

PROBLEMS WITH THE PRODUCT

Are they in the right order? No. The order's wrong because if your reader has no idea what an energy drink is or does, she won't be able to fully understand the market. So shift that category to the top of the chunk.

Next, put the categories in chronological order. Put the history of the market first, then what it's like today. Finally, finish with the reasons for the product's success, as that speaks directly to the chunk's bottom line—that this market bursts with potential.

What about PROBLEMS WITH THE PRODUCT? This is one short detail in your actual notes, about the medicinal taste of energy drinks. When you evaluate it now, it doesn't seem to fit. Even if consumers complain about the taste of energy drinks, they're still buying them. If you were writing a detailed plan showing how you intend to formulate Brainstorm, you might include this detail and promise that your brand will taste loads better. But since you're not doing that here, this detail drops away. Not everything you pick up in your research will be included in your final piece of writing.

Look next at Development 2. At the moment, it holds three categories:

CURRENT TARGET MARKET

MARKETING IN CURRENT MARKET

UNSERVED CONSUMERS

Are they in the right order? CURRENT TARGET MARKET does set the context for what's out there, as does how the market leaders are trying to reach that market. The reader needs both these pieces of context before she can fully appreciate the group you point to as your "unserved consumers." On the level of broad categories, Development 2 looks good. And so far, so does Development 3. We move there from introducing our product to talking about marketing it. It wouldn't make sense to discuss marketing a product the reader doesn't recognize.

With our three Developments in general order, it's time to turn to the Problem and Resolution chunks. What will fill them?

In this case, the point of the Problem is to assert that a new product can help the company grow. If that's so, you need to say, up front, what that new product is and how it might help business. You'll do this briefly, enough to whet the reader's appetite to see more. Therefore, simply make a note to yourself to introduce the idea that Brainstorm is a new product that will help the company grow—in other words, to write a sentence or two that will make the point your Problem statement directs you to make.

What about our Resolution? This will be the place to sum up our new idea—Brainstorm. It would be nice to give the reader a picture of the product in some way. Therefore, add the category THE BRAINSTORM PRODUCT here, too, and make yourself a note about summing up and "seeing" the product. Now, before you lay the actual notes in place, separate those labeled THE BRAINSTORM PRODUCT into two. Put those that help you "see" the new product as it will look to the consumer in the Resolution, and keep those that show how it will be created in Development 3. Finally, add the category NEXT STEP to the Resolution, as this is the place to prod our reader to take (or authorize) action. Our outline now looks this way, with notes substituted for categories:

Problem: Brainstorm offers growth.

Development 1 (Background): Market bursts with potential.

Development 2 (Bridge): Geniuses create a market.

Development 3 (Point of Insight): Plan shows how we'll succeed.

Resolution: Brainstorm will succeed because it serves a different kind of consumer.

Introduce Brainstorm and assert that it will help the company grow by tapping into the energy drink market.

Problem: Brainstorm offers growth.

Red Bull active ingredients—taurine and vitamins added to caffeine and other ingredients. **WHAT ARE ENERGY DRINKS?**

Energy drinks sell for $2 for an 8-ounce can. **WHAT ARE ENERGY DRINKS?**

Energy drinks are mildly carbonated. **WHAT ARE ENERGY DRINKS?**

Early energy drinks: Jolt, Red Bull. **HISTORY OF THE MARKET**

Jolt, created 1985, was soda with more caffeine. **HISTORY OF THE MARKET**

Red Bull, created 1987, took Japanese energy drinks and marketed them to Western consumers. **HISTORY OF THE MARKET**

Red Bull is market leader—has 60 percent market share. **THE MARKET TODAY**

Last year energy drinks sold $1.1 billion in U.S. market. **THE MARKET TODAY**

Market has grown 700 percent in the last five years; still growing. **THE MARKET TODAY**

Pepsi and Coke introduced energy drinks this year to same sports-oriented market. **THE MARKET TODAY**

Energy drink market can still grow. Today it's only 2 percent of the $60 billion soft drink market. **THE MARKET TODAY**

Success attributed to marketing. **REASON FOR PRODUCT SUCCESS**

Development 1 (Background): Market bursts with potential.

Young men are target market. **CURRENT TARGET MARKET**

Market also targets hip hop fans and video game users. **CURRENT TARGET MAR-KET**

Energy drink companies usually sponsor extreme sports events to attract consumers. **MARKETING IN CURRENT MARKET**

Red Bull sponsorships: **MARKETING IN CURRENT MARKET**

paraglider across the Grand Canyon **MARKETING IN CURRENT MARKET**

homemade aircraft flying **MARKETING IN CURRENT MARKET**

Go Fast! plans to sponsor a skydiver in a wing suit; no parachute. **MARKETING IN CURRENT MARKET**

Other marketing sponsorships by drink-makers: snowboarding, bridge jumping, rocket launches. **MARKETING IN CURRENT MARKET**

"Geniuses" need energy to stay up late, studying and creating. **UNSERVED CONSUMERS**

Who are they? Teens and adults, men and women in science, engineering, computers, art, music, dance. **UNSERVED CONSUMERS**

Development 2 (Bridge): Geniuses create a market.

Add extra dose of pyridoxine (B$_6$), said to boost creativity, as our special ingredient. **THE BRAINSTORM PRODUCT**

Brainstorm could come in both sugar and sugar-free versions. It would be highly carbonated to "pop" with creativity. **THE BRAINSTORM PRODUCT**

Marketing ideas:

Taste tests with memory tests **HOW TO REACH THE BRAINSTORM CONSUMER**

Computer game tournaments **HOW TO REACH THE BRAINSTORM CONSUMER**

Alternative music festivals **HOW TO REACH THE BRAINSTORM CONSUMER**

Campus art/music/poetry promotions **HOW TO REACH THE BRAINSTORM CONSUMER**

Engineering design contests **HOW TO REACH THE BRAINSTORM CONSUMER**

"Can you get in?" marketing idea—consumers take IQ tests to prove they can "drink the drink." **HOW TO REACH THE BRAINSTORM CONSUMER**

Brainstorm tagline: "Carbonate your inner genius." **HOW TO REACH THE BRAINSTORM CONSUMER**

Development 3 (Point of Insight): Plan shows how we'll succeed.

Sum up the arguments for Brainstorm, and let the reader "see" the Brainstorm product.

Brainstorm could be marketed in a lightbulb-shaped can, to highlight its "genius" focus. **THE BRAINSTORM PRODUCT**

Possibly sell Brainstorm for slightly less than other energy drinks (use smaller bottles like soda makers do) and gain advantage that way. **THE BRAINSTORM PRODUCT**

Next step: analyze startup costs for this project. **NEXT STEP**

Resolution: Brainstorm will succeed because it serves a different kind of consumer.

Again, with notes in place, evaluate each chunk of the List Outline:

- Does the logic hold together? Does each point lead smoothly to the next?
- Do all the points drive toward the bottom line of that chunk?
- Is anything missing?

Here's what you find:

1. In Development 1, we want to begin by defining energy drinks and then move into the history of the market. Therefore, pull out the ingredients of Red Bull—common to most energy drinks—and keep those on top, but put anything distinct about Red Bull, such as the fact that it differs from colas—into the part of the chunk (the middle section) where we discuss the market's history. Since Red Bull's success is generally attributed to its innovative marketing, that should go next. Follow that with the entry of the market leaders into the fray— Pepsi and Coke. And to hit the bull's-eye of the chunk's bottom line, end with the fantastic growth the market has seen and the growth it still can see.

2. The information in Development 3 is slightly out of order. This Development has the crucial job of introducing Brainstorm, but at the moment, it does that very suddenly, starting with Brainstorm's ingredients. A better opening would be to introduce the tagline, "Carbonate your inner genius," and then explain what the product is and how it would be marketed. Finally, this important development should end with its own mini-conclusion that emphasizes the possibilities of the market and shows the plan's viability—the chunk's bottom line. This will also serve as a transition into the Resolution.

3. In the Resolution, the note that the company's next step would be to analyze start-up costs currently comes last. That's a weak way to end when you've been barreling toward the point of what a success Brainstorm would be. Move it up to the top of the Development, possibly slipping it into the transition that will open the chunk.

So much for what's there. What about what's not there?

It would probably be nice to quantify the genius consumer somehow. As it stands, the reader has no idea how many people we might be talking about. This gap—which exists in Development 2—can't be fixed by reorganizing the notes we've got. It calls for a second pass at research. But never fear, once you're this far into the outline process, you won't have to do the kind of research you did earlier. This time, you head straight for what you need, so you can get it quickly.

DIRECTED RESEARCH

Don't allow yourself to get lost in mounds of new information. Write your question down and then go find the answer. To speed the process, consider the following tips:

- Whether your source is online or in hard copy, skim. Search indexes and tables of contents for your specific subject. When you find it, skim the text looking for what you need.

- Employ search engines. Ask your question directly and see if the computer can hand you the answer.
- Don't ignore government agencies. If it's a statistic you're looking for, they're full of them.
- Look to university libraries online or on the phone. If your question is not too specialized, librarians can often help.
- Ask. If your topic is narrow and your question specific, someone you work with might know the answer and save you lots of time. Half the work is figuring out the right question. Don't be afraid to look for help with the answers.

In Development 2, we want to know the size of the "genius" market. While no one actually counts people that way, it *is* possible to discover the number of young people in the right age range. Check the latest U.S. Census, available to anyone online. A quick check shows that according to the latest count, 27 million eighteen- to twenty-four-year-olds were living (and presumably staying up late and getting thirsty) in America. If Brainstorm attracted even a drop of that large pool, you could expect a big bonus next year.

Step 9: Add Transitions and an Opening Hook

As in our Caesar proposal, the Brainstorm piece's transitions will be both "regular" and "super-sized." They'll make small connections from one idea to the next in the middle of chunks, but they'll also, in the opening and sometimes the closing of a section, serve as a mini-introduction or conclusion, keeping the overall theme of the piece—the big bottom line—front and center for the reader.

In this case, you can find material for these super-sized transitions by searching through the notes already organized in your outline sections.

In Development 1, for example, we've shown the reader that energy drinks are very, very hot. Now we're heading into a discussion of marketing, which will wind up with the point that "geniuses" offer a potential new consumer. What kind of transition will connect those two chunks, while reminding the reader of our product, Brainstorm?

How about something like this: "Brainstorm's potential comes from the fact that for the most part, the energy drink market focuses on young males."

This transition does its connecting job—it mentions the energy drink market we've just explored, and it mentions potential, which we're about to explore. But it also highlights Brainstorm, pulling our ultimate bottom line right back into the spotlight.

THE OPENING HOOK

Until now, we've discussed opening hooks mainly in terms of quickly setting context, or even simply as a salutation at the opening of a letter. But in complex and creative pieces like our Brainstorm proposal, the opening hook will take on a whole new meaning.

In this context, if your regular transition is a traffic cop, and your supersized transition is the chief of police, then the narrative hook is a superhero. That's so because it carries a supernaturally heavy load. It must capture the reader's attention, orient her, and get her curious enough to ask the question that will drive toward your Resolution.

The opening hook accomplishes this feat in the same way Clark Kent always did—it has two personalities, one mild-mannered, one dressed in red cape and tights.

The Mild-Mannered Opening Hook: Context

A context hook works nine to five, shops the sales, and is, above all, *reliable*. Its job is to orient the reader by welcoming her into the piece with a list of the things she'll need to know: the what, where, when, and who of the subject at hand.

To write a context hook for our Brainstorm piece, call Clark Kent. Simply follow the direction of the note you left in that chunk earlier:

> Introduce Brainstorm and assert that it will help the company grow by tapping into the energy drink market.

Problem: A new product, Brainstorm, could offer Get Me a Drink, Inc., a way into the lucrative energy drink market.

Try something like this, using your most basic research on the general market: "This proposal offers Get Me a Drink, Inc., a way into the lucrative energy drink market. The current market leaders promote energy drinks almost exclusively to young men. Our proposed product, Brainstorm, would target a new market by creating a drink that could boost not only energy, but creativity."

Well done, Clark! The reader now knows that the energy market is lucrative, that it's narrowly focused, and that the idea being proposed, Brainstorm, could create a niche for Get Me a Drink, Inc. Since growth is the reader's concern, this statement ought to get her asking: "How would this work? Tell me more!"

If you chose this type of hook, it would essentially take care of the entire Problem section. You wouldn't need much more. But you do have another option. You can turn Clark Kent into Superman.

The Grabber Opening Hook

A grabber opening hook doesn't walk in and shake hands, adjust its glasses, and say, "Excuse me, Chief, can I talk to you for a second?" It dashes out of the nearest phone booth at the speed of sound. When Superman zooms past, people don't need to orient themselves, they simply pay attention. *Then* they orient themselves. Grabber opening hooks delay the necessary orientation job by making a big enough splash so that readers are *in*. Once you've got them, you continue by explaining where exactly *in* is.

To develop a grabber opening hook for our Brainstorm proposal, we'd build on the context we've already developed above. But we'd also look through our notes for a compelling piece of information, an anecdote or statistic that could grab the reader's attention and swiftly pique her interest.

Glancing through the notes, you can see we have a sharp statistic like that in Development 1, as part of our background on the current energy drink market. That's where we've got numbers on annual sales in the market, plus the market's rate of growth. Pull that piece up, add it to what you already have, and you've got the reader's attention with a grabber opening hook: "Americans spend $1.1 billion on energy drinks a year and almost all of those profits are generated by a relatively small segment of the market: young men who like extreme sports. Even with this limited focus, market analysts estimate the industry has grown 700 percent in the past five years."

Once the reader's focused on this lucrative energy drink market, you could move on to provide the rest of the context: "This proposal offers Get Me a Drink, Inc., a way into this lucrative market. Our proposed product, Brainstorm, would target a new market by creating a drink that could boost not only energy, but creativity."

Here, Superman does more for us than Clark Kent. Of course, a grabber opening hook is not *always* the right choice. You wouldn't want Superman showing up at the *Daily Planet* reporting the news. Use Clark where appropriate, and Superman where possible.

Step 10: Polish Your Draft

Once you've connected all the dots—added transitions both internally and at the opening (and sometimes closing) of each chunk—most of your drafting work will be done. It's here, in a high-level proposal like this one, where *listening* to your draft—reading it out loud—pays off. Put longer sentences at the opening of chunks, where you introduce material; shorten your sentences as you near each mini bottom line. By paying attention to the rhythm of sentences, you'll give your proposal maximum power.

Take a look at the draft, with headings, transitions, and polish complete:

To: Bubbles McGee, President, Get Me a Drink, Inc.

From: I. M. Brainy, Research & Development

(grabber opening hook) Americans spend $1.1 billion on energy drinks a year and almost all of those profits are generated by a relatively small segment of the market: young men who like extreme sports. Even with this limited focus, market analysts estimate the industry has grown 700 percent in the past five years.

It's time for Get Me a Drink, Inc., with its solid reputation for high-quality health drinks, to reach for a piece of this market. We are in an excellent position to take advantage of surging popular demand for energy drinks—but only if we can find a niche as yet unserved by existing brands. To fill that need, I'm proposing a new drink called "Brainstorm," which, with its tagline, "Carbonate your inner genius," will target a segment of the market that has been all but ignored by today's popular energy drink makers: women, intellectuals, and "creative types" who need to stay up late to burn the midnight oil.

PROBLEM: BRAINSTORM OFFERS GROWTH.

What are energy drinks?

(major transition) Energy drinks succeed so fabulously because Americans don't get enough sleep, and they like products with edge. Americans are also health-conscious, competitive, and thirsty. Commonly defined as beverages that claim to offer an energy boost with active, unregulated ingredients, energy drinks include caffeine, but also the B-complex vitamins, glucose, and even taurine, an amino acid said to enhance the effects of caffeine. Energy drinks differ from colas both in the stimulants they provide and in their less-intense carbonation.

The earliest modern "energy" drink in this country was Jolt, created in 1985, and marketed as a cola with "all the sugar and twice the caffeine." But Jolt did not jumpstart the market in the way Austrian-based Red Bull did, two years later. Red Bull introduced a product distinct from cola, mildly carbonated and enhanced by additives. The company's greatest innovation, however, was its marketing strategy. With aggressive and innovative promotions, Red Bull created the energy drink market by appealing to extreme sport fans. It continues to dominate today with almost 60 percent market share. That may soon end; this year both Pepsi and Coke launched competing brands: AMP and Full Throttle.

Despite the fierce competition, energy drinks are poised to make a lot more money: today, they make up only 2 percent of the $60 billion carbonated soft drink market, a number that could balloon if energy drinks could reach beyond their core market of young male consumers to a broader consumer base.
D1: MARKET BURSTS WITH POTENTIAL.

Brainstorm's Potential

(major transition) Brainstorm's potential comes from the fact that for the most part, the energy drink market focuses on young males. Energy drink makers generally ignore traditional TV and radio advertising in favor of attention-getting publicity stunts that appeal to fans of extreme sports.

Recent energy drink marketing has included a Red Bull paraglider crossing the Grand Canyon and a plan by Go Fast! to sponsor a skydiver who will leap from a plane wearing only a winged jumpsuit—no parachute. Snowboarding, bridge jumping, and rocket launches—these and other extreme sports grab consumers' attention far more than advertising through traditional media.
(transition) But young men are not the only group that could benefit from energy drinks. According to the latest census, there are almost 27 million 18–24 year olds in America, and not all of them like extreme sports.
(transition) Who, then, is left out of the equation? Women, and non–sports or non–mainstream music fans, a group we'll label the "genius" types—anyone

from budding musicians to computer engineers. The young genius market includes those creative teens and young adults whose drive is mental, not physical. Staying up late to study, invent, write music, and create art, they need an energy boost as much, if not more, than athletes. It's this unserved market that could generate the next big breakthrough in the energy drink arena.

D2: GENIUSES CREATE A MARKET.

(major transition) Enter Brainstorm, with its tagline: "Carbonate your inner genius." As envisioned, Brainstorm—in both sugar and sugar-free versions—would be highly carbonated. Most energy drinks are mildly carbonated, to reflect their sports-drink orientation. But Brainstorm would be closer to soda, with the added boost of energy enhancers like the B-complex vitamins and, of course, caffeine. Brainstorm's special ingredient would be an extra dose of pyridoxine (B_6), reputed to heighten creativity. With its extra "pop" of carbonation and its special creativity ingredient, the product would stand apart.

Most important, Brainstorm could be marketed in all sorts of creative and totally new ways. Get Me a Drink, Inc., could sponsor:

• Taste tests combined with memory tests

• Alternative music festivals, "Dungeons and Dragons" type computer tournaments

• Mad scientist contests (Go Fast! sponsored someone jumping out of a plane; we could sponsor someone designing one.)

• A Brainstorm "poet of the month," "musician of the month," and "novelist of the month" on college campuses

• A "can you get in?" promotion, where consumers who scored high enough on "IQ" tests would prove they could "drink the drink."

(major transition) Brainstorm could also be marketed to the big computer companies for all their engineers, to college students before midterms and finals, and to the schools of design and art around the country. Because the market is so untapped, the possibilities are very nearly endless.

D3: PLAN SHOWS HOW WE'LL SUCCEED.

(major transition) To pursue this project, our next step would be to analyze the start-up costs involved. But Brainstorm already has the built-in benefit of the market it's entering. Energy drinks can be advertised more cheaply than traditional soft drinks, and yet they sell for significantly more than cola, at an average of $2 for an 8-ounce can. The Brainstorm can could be shaped like a lightbulb, to give consumers an instant message. If we made our cans slightly smaller than average, we could also offer Brainstorm at a comparably reduced price, to further entice our targeted consumer to buy it.

If even one element of this diverse "genius" market responded to the creative look, makeup, and marketing of this product, Brainstorm would be an instant success.

RESOLUTION: BRAINSTORM WILL SUCCEED BECAUSE IT SERVES A DIFFERENT KIND OF CONSUMER.

CHAPTER 10

HOW-TO MANUALS

Of all forms of writing, how-to manuals require the most precision when it comes to organizing details. How-to writing applies when you're writing a set of directions, setting out a list of requirements, or teaching a system. Simple how-to's are best approached like a recipe—they rely on strict chronological order. You can't mix the batter until you've broken the eggs. However, audience is also crucial in how-to writing. How much the reader already knows dictates the steps you will need to teach him.

Intent: The intent of a how-to manual is to:

- Explain why a system works
- Show the reader how it works
- Teach the reader to do it

Some how-to's simply teach the system without explaining it. These provide only a set of directions—for example, how to put together a dresser or install a program on your computer. More complex how-to's let readers in on *why* the system works, sharing theory or background to help them better grasp the tools they will be learning to use.

Bottom Line: The bottom line of a how-to manual is to:

- Teach the reader a system

The System in 10 Easy Steps

You are Ursula, the snake lady at Top Hat Traveling Circus. Binky, your beloved (but temperamental) 150-pound Burmese python, is your pride and joy. Unfortunately, you're needed out of town to tend to a family emergency, and Binky doesn't travel well. To see he's fed while you're away, write a how-to manual for your fellow circus workers. Your goal is to keep Binky (and the circus workers) healthy while you're gone.

Step 1: Questions and Research

1. **Who is my audience?** Pokey, Martha, Anthea, and Rooney, the circus workers assigned to Binky while you're out of town.
2. **What do they want to know?** How to feed Binky and live to tell the tale.
3. **What is my bottom line point?** (see below)

Find out:

- What Binky eats
- How to prepare Binky's food
- How to feed Binky
- What *not* to do

Step 2: Evaluate Your Notes and Determine the Bottom Line

Binky likes live food (rabbits, chickens). But frozen is best.

Order from www.prey4it.com.

Standard order—1 pack full-grown rabbits, once a month. (Ask for Jerry.)

Store rabbits in Mrs. Evans's freezer (ignore tirade).

Binky eats every other Wednesday evening. Allow full day for thawing and prep.

Binky's eyes (and mouth) are bigger than his stomach. Feed him prey no bigger than his wide middle. (Don't let Jerry talk you into small pigs—rabbits keep Binky trim, pigs make him obese.)

Don't worry if rabbit looks too big for his mouth—his mouth stretches.

Don't let painted lady near Binky. She still hasn't forgiven him for what happened to her cat.

Binky sees anything small and moving as food. So two (tall) people should feed Binky.

Binky is a fussy eater. Dip rabbit in chicken broth after warming. Binky likes chicken, but it's bad for his digestion.

Defrost rabbit four hours, then warm in water or with blow dryer.

Don't use microwave—Mrs. Evans hates when prey explodes.

Do not overheat rabbit—Binky won't eat cooked food.

Dangle rabbit in front of Binky—use tongs, not hand! (Binky sometimes gets confused as to what he's meant to eat.)

Let Binky strike and grab prey, then coil around it.

Give Binky privacy.

Make sure you re-lock the cage.

Don't bother Binky for at least a week. He's a slow digester.

The bottom line? Feed Binky very carefully and we'll all end up happy.

Step 3: Identify the Problem and Resolution

Remember that audience is key here. Your circus worker friends want to know how to feed the snake, but they don't want him eating just any old food (Pokey or Anthea, for example). Therefore, your Problem and Resolution should address both concerns.

You say:

Problem: Binky needs careful feeding.

Resolution: Feed Binky *this* way.

The reader says:

How can I feed him and not become food?

Gotcha. I'll follow this guide to the letter!

Step 4: Categorize Your Notes

Binky likes live food (rabbits, chickens). But frozen is best. **EQUIPMENT**

Order from www.prey4it.com. **EQUIPMENT**

Standard order—1 pack full-grown rabbits, once a month. (Ask for Jerry.) **EQUIPMENT**

Store rabbits in Mrs. Evans's freezer (ignore tirade). **PREPARATION**

Binky eats every other Wednesday evening. Allow full day for thawing and prep. **PREPARATION**

Binky's eyes (and mouth) are bigger than his stomach. Feed him prey no bigger than his wide middle. Don't let Jerry talk you into small pigs—rabbits keep Binky trim, pigs make him obese. **EQUIPMENT**

Don't worry if rabbit looks too big for his mouth—his mouth stretches. **EQUIPMENT**

Don't let painted lady near Binky. She still hasn't forgiven him for what happened to her cat. **WARNINGS**

Binky sees anything small and moving as food. So two (tall) people should feed Binky. **WARNINGS**

Binky is a fussy eater. Dip rabbit in chicken broth after warming. Binky likes chicken, but it's bad for his digestion. **PREPARATION**

Defrost rabbit four hours, then warm in water or with blow dryer. **PREPARATION**

Don't use microwave—Mrs. Evans hates when prey explodes. **WARNINGS**

Do not overheat rabbit—Binky won't eat cooked food. **PREPARATION**

Dangle rabbit in front of Binky—use tongs, not hand! (Binky sometimes gets confused as to what he's meant to eat.) **FEEDING**

Let Binky strike and grab prey, then coil around it. **FEEDING**

Give Binky privacy. **FEEDING**

Make sure you re-lock the cage. **FEEDING**

Don't bother Binky for at least a week. He's a slow digester. **AFTER FEEDING**

Step 5: Choose Development 3—Point of Insight

Here are our categories:

EQUIPMENT

PREPARATION

WARNINGS

FEEDING

AFTER FEEDING

Which category will show readers that they can successfully feed Binky? Only the notes labeled FEEDING—which show your circus pals how to get the food into Binky's exceptionally large mouth, without following it down there themselves. The bottom line? Learn how to entice the snake to eat the right food, or invite Binky to dinner.

You say:

Problem: Binky needs careful
   feeding.

Development 1 (Background):

Development 2 (Bridge):

Development 3 (Point of Insight):

Invite Binky to dinner.

Resolution: Feed Binky *this* way.

The reader says:

How can I feed him and not become
   food?

Oh, tongs! That's a relief!

Gotcha. I'll follow this guide to
   the letter!

Step 6: Choose Development 1—Background

EQUIPMENT

PREPARATION

WARNINGS

FEEDING **D3**

AFTER FEEDING

What background must your fellow circus performers have in order to successfully begin this process? The first step in almost any process involves assembling the right equipment. If your friends haven't ordered the frozen entrée, Binky will have nothing suitable to eat. Therefore, our notes labeled EQUIPMENT will make up D1. Its bottom line is simply order Binky's food.

You say:		The reader says:
Problem: Binky needs carefully feeding.		*How can I feed him and not become food?*
Development 1 (Background): Order Binky's food.		*Talk to Jerry. No pigs. Check.*
Development 2 (Bridge):		
Development 3 (Point of Insight): Invite Binky to dinner.		*Oh, tongs! That's a relief!*
Resolution: Feed Binky *this* way.		*Gotcha. I'll follow this guide to the letter!*

Step 7: Choose Development 2—Bridge

EQUIPMENT **D1**

PREPARATION

WARNINGS

FEEDING **D3**

AFTER FEEDING

Your friends have got the equipment, and they know how to feed Binky. What happens between buying frozen prey and dangling it before the python? How-to's work in strict chronological order. Think of them as a recipe and you can't go wrong. You've had your readers assemble the ingredients and showed them how to serve the meal. The bridge that connects those two is preparing the food. Thus, our notes labeled PREPARATION make up Development 2. Its bottom line is prepare Binky's meal.

You say:		The reader says:
Problem: Binky needs careful feeding.		*How can I feed him and not become food?*
Development 1 (Background): Order Binky's food.		*Talk to Jerry. No pigs.* *Check.*
Development 2 (Bridge): **Prepare Binky's meal.**		*No microwave. Understood.*
Development 3 (Point of Insight): Invite Binky to dinner.		*Oh, tongs! That's a relief!*
Resolution: Feed Binky *this* way.		*Gotcha. I'll follow this guide to the letter!*

Step 8: Create a List Outline—Organize Categories and Details

EQUIPMENT **D1**

PREPARATION **D2**

WARNINGS

FEEDING **D3**

AFTER FEEDING

Organizing a system doesn't pose the challenge other writing does. Proposals, and even many reports, require you to think about which ideas hold the greatest power to bring your reader to your point of view. Instructional writing only asks that you determine which steps come first in a given process. If you've used that process yourself—and know it well enough—this should be fairly obvious.

In our snake how-to guide, the power of chronological organization is clear. We've used our categories EQUIPMENT, PREPARATION, and FEEDING. The notes on AFTER FEEDING clearly belong in the Resolution, simply based on time order. WARNINGS, however, can be tricky. Though they are a category in notes, they belong tied to the steps where they'll be most useful. Therefore, pair each warning with the correct outline category. Warnings related to preparation, like the fact that you shouldn't heat frozen rabbit in a microwave, belong with PREPARATION in Development 2. Warnings related to the painted lady and her grudge against Binky probably belong at the moment when the cage will be opened—that is, feeding time. Look below at our List Outline, first with categories and then with notes, to see the progression of our how-to document:

Target Outline:

Problem: Binky needs careful feeding.
Development 1 (Background): Order Binky's food.
Development 2 (Bridge): Prepare Binky's meal.
Development 3 (Point of Insight): Invite Binky to dinner.
Resolution: Feed Binky *this* way.

Problem: Binky needs careful feeding.

EQUIPMENT

Development 1 (Background): Order Binky's food.

PREPARATION
WARNINGS

Development 2 (Bridge): Prepare Binky's meal.

```
┌─────────────────────────────────────────────────────┐
│                      FEEDING                          │
│                     WARNINGS                          │
└─────────────────────────────────────────────────────┘
                        ▼
```

Development 3 (Point of Insight): Invite Binky to dinner.

```
┌─────────────────────────────────────────────────────┐
│                  AFTER FEEDING                        │
└─────────────────────────────────────────────────────┘
                        ▼
```

Resolution: Feed Binky *this* way.

What about our empty Problem section? Generally, open a how-to guide with a short introduction explaining the overall goal of the process and any important warnings or precautions that apply to the whole system. With a note inserted in the Problem section and our warnings added in the right places, look now at the revised List Outline:

```
┌─────────────────────────────────────────────────────┐
│ Feeding Binky requires love and care. An undernourished Binky is a cranky Binky. │
│    Follow instructions carefully to keep everyone safe and happy.  │
└─────────────────────────────────────────────────────┘
                        ▼
```

Problem: Binky needs careful feeding.

```
┌─────────────────────────────────────────────────────┐
│ Binky likes live food (rabbits, chickens). But frozen is best. EQUIPMENT │
│ Order from www.prey4it.com. EQUIPMENT                 │
│ Standard order—1 pack full-grown rabbits, once a month. (Ask for Jerry.) EQUIP- │
│    MENT                                               │
│ Binky's eyes (and mouth) are bigger than his stomach. Feed him prey no bigger than │
│    his wide middle. Don't let Jerry talk you into small pigs—rabbits keep Binky trim, │
│    pigs make him obese. EQUIPMENT                     │
└─────────────────────────────────────────────────────┘
                        ▼
```

Development 1 (Background): Order Binky's food.

> *Store rabbits in Mrs. Evans's freezer (ignore tirade).* **PREPARATION**
>
> *Binky eats every other Wednesday evening. Allow full day for thawing and prep.* **PREPARATION**
>
> *Binky is a fussy eater. Dip rabbit in chicken broth after warming. Binky likes chicken, but it's bad for his digestion.* **PREPARATION**
>
> *Defrost rabbit four hours, then warm in water or with blow dryer.* **PREPARATION**
>
> *Don't use microwave—Mrs. Evans hates when prey explodes.* **WARNINGS**
>
> *Do not overheat rabbit—Binky won't eat cooked food.* **PREPARATION**

⬇

Development 2 (Bridge): Prepare Binky's meal.

> *Don't let painted lady near Binky. She still hasn't forgiven him for what happened to her cat.* **WARNINGS**
>
> *Binky sees anything small and moving as food. So two (tall) people should feed Binky.* **WARNINGS**
>
> *Dangle rabbit in front of Binky—use tongs, not hand! (Binky sometimes gets confused as to what he's meant to eat.)* **FEEDING**
>
> *Let Binky strike and grab prey, then coil around it.* **FEEDING**
>
> *Give Binky privacy.* **FEEDING**
>
> *Make sure you re-lock the cage.* **FEEDING**

⬇

Development 3 (Point of Insight): Invite Binky to dinner.

> *Don't bother Binky for at least a week. He's a slow digester.* **AFTER FEEDING**

⬇

Resolution: Feed Binky *this* way.

Step 9: Add Transitions and an Opening Hook

How-to transitions tend to be time-based, since how-to guides work in chronological order. "Next," "Step 2," or simply a bulleted or numbered list provide transitions in a how-to. When the chronology is obvious enough, simply beginning a new paragraph will offer enough of a transition, as you'll see in the following draft.

The guide's opening hook will be based on its audience. As Ursula, you can write a chatty opening to your circus friends, or simply begin with a no-nonsense "Step 1."

Step 10: Polish Your Draft

Polishing a how-to is at least as important as polishing any other piece. Make sure your reader can move easily from sentence to sentence and step to step. Avoid words that will stop him, that he won't understand or will have to look up. Keep sentences simple enough that the content, and not the intricate phraseology, leaves the impression. And always use white space and headings to help guide the reader through the text.

As your guide to feeding Binky is written to close colleagues, you should address them by name. And since the circus is just one big happy family, it's fine to pepper this guide with chatty asides and explanations in parentheses. Formal guides should stick to straightforward instructions and limit commentary.

Below, read through the Feeding Binky How-To Guide:

(opening hook) Dear Pokey, Martha, Anthea, and Rooney,

Feeding Binky requires love and careful handling. Keeping him well fed is very important because if he's undernourished, Binky gets extremely cranky. Though he can be temperamental and a fussy eater, with good preparation and the right food, you'll do fine.

PROBLEM: BINKY NEEDS FEEDING.

(transition) Despite Magnifico's nasty rumor-mongering, Binky does not, as a rule, eat the rabbits out of the magician's hat (though they can of course be used in an emergency). He prefers live rabbits and chickens, but I feed him frozen, pre-killed prey, which I order from www.prey4it.com. My standard order is a package of full-grown rabbits, once a month. Talk to Jerry—he knows me there.

Do not let Jerry convince you to order small pigs. Rabbits keep Binky trim, and the pigs make him obese. Binky's eyes (and mouth) are bigger than his stomach, but he actually can't digest anything wider than his middle. If you try to feed him something big, he'll swallow it and bring it back a few days later. Don't, however, worry if the rabbit looks too big for Binky's mouth. Binky's mouth stretches.

DEVELOPMENT 1: ORDER BINKY'S FOOD.

I use the big freezer to store the rabbits. They're very hygienically packaged, and don't believe a word Mrs. Evans says if she tells you they sometimes get mixed up with dinner. They're clearly labeled and it isn't true.

Binky eats every other Wednesday evening. You'll need to begin preparing his meal in the morning. Thaw one or two frozen rabbits for about four hours. Do not attempt to speed this process by using Mrs. Evans's microwave. Microwaved rabbits can explode, and I do not want my salary docked again.

Warm the thawed rabbit in water or with a blow dryer, so Binky will think it's alive. Be careful not to overheat the rabbit, as Binky will not eat cooked food.

If Binky seems fussy, try dipping the rabbit in chicken broth to make him eat it. Binky loves chicken, but it's bad for his digestion.

DEVELOPMENT 2: PREPARE BINKY'S MEAL.

(transition) Feeding

Binky should always be fed by at least two people. I recommend that Rooney and Martha do the actual feeding, as they're both tall. Binky sometimes mistakes anything small and moving for food, and it would be terrible to have a repeat of that unfortunate incident with Mini Marty, the short clown.

To feed Binky, use the tongs that hang on the side of his enclosure. Dangle the rabbit so it looks as if it's moving. Don't use your hand (Binky sometimes takes a bigger than average first bite) and please don't let the painted lady dart in while you're feeding him—she still hasn't forgiven him for what happened to her cat.

If you keep the lights low and dangle the rabbit near his head, Binky should make a sudden strike. Once he's got hold of the rabbit, wait while he coils himself around it, then close and lock the cage.

DEVELOPMENT 3: INVITE BINKY TO DINNER.

Binky needs privacy while he eats. Leave him alone for at least a week after feeding. Binky is a slow digester.

Thanks for all your help and for taking good care of Binky!

Ursula

RESOLUTION: FEED BINKY *THIS* WAY.

CHAPTER 11

HOW THE EXPERTS DO IT

Whether they know it or not, all effective business writers use the Target Outline. They've undoubtedly not moved through the process the way we have, but they nevertheless produce a piece that raises a Problem, moves through three Developments, and ultimately resolves the reader's question with a single, overarching bottom line. That's because the Target Outline is the easiest way to learn what all good writers know: how to get—and keep—the reader's attention.

Below, instead of moving through our process as usual, we're going to look first at a polished piece—published a few years ago by Procter & Gamble. The writers there are among the best in the business, and we'll analyze their piece to see how they applied all the rules of good structure—including the use of complex transitions—to write an introduction to the company's annual report to shareholders.

P&G BRANDS: WINNING THE WORLD'S CONSUMERS

"Everything we do is focused on building our brands," says P&G Chairman and Chief Executive Ed Artzt. That should come as no surprise, because Procter & Gamble is a company of brands—more than 300, in fact, marketed in over 140 countries. What makes P&G unique is not just the unparalleled number of leading brands our Company markets, but the enduring loyalty consumers have to our brands—across generations and geographies.

"Brand loyalty is the foundation of our business," Artzt says. "A new mother has to decide what brand of diapers to buy every week. Most consumers buy a box of laundry detergent 10 or 12 times a year. And every one of these purchase decisions is an opportunity to switch to another brand.

"But over the years, the consistent quality and value of our products have kept people coming back to Pampers, Ivory, Crest, Ariel and dozens of other P&G brands."

"We work hard to provide that superior quality and value day in and day out," says President John Pepper. "It means we must continually adapt to changing consumer needs."

Understanding Consumer Needs

"In fact," Pepper adds, "the most important thing we do is to understand what consumers are looking for from a brand—and then consistently meet their needs with products of superior quality and value." This is true in every market where our brands are sold, from the United States to the United Kingdom and from Mexico to China.

Artzt agrees. "Consumers have to trust that a brand will meet *all* their needs, all the time. That requires superior product technology, and it also requires a sufficient breadth of product choices. We should never give consumers a product reason to switch away from one of our brands."

Executive Vice President Durk Jager explains. "People can have a wide range of needs within a given category.

"A woman who uses Olay, for example, may need a face wash product first thing in the morning, a UV protectant during the day, and a replenishing cream at night. We make sure she can meet all those needs with one brand— Oil of Olay."

Our commitment to these principles—delivering superior products that meet a range of consumer needs—is a key reason why consumers remain loyal to so many P&G brands.

Creating Loyalty from the Start

Another way we create and build consumer loyalty is by attracting consumers the first time they purchase a product in one of our categories. "When new parents buy their first diapers, we want them to reach for Pampers," says Pepper.

To attract consumers at this "point of market entry," we must offer the right quality product at the right price.

"For example," says Pepper, "in some countries where incomes are low, striking this balance between quality and price requires us to market a diaper that offers more basic features, at a substantially lower price, than the premium diaper we sell in many countries."

The needs of consumers may vary from country to country, but the principle remains the same, as Artzt explains: "By winning consumer loyalty at this crucial decision point, we have the best opportunity to keep their loyalty for the long term." This focus on building consumer loyalty early is an important strategy for many P&G brands, including Always, Cover Girl and Clearasil.

Building Loyalty with Advertising

Our leading brands begin with world-class product technology, but it's advertising that gets consumers' attention and persuades them to use our products again and again.

"Advertising is the lifeblood of our brands," says Artzt, who points to Pantene Pro-V and Vicks VapoRub as recent examples of "products that became world brands on the strength of technology backed up by world-class advertising."

"We use advertising to tell consumers what our brands stand for," Jager adds. "And to show them why and how our brands will meet their needs. And we know it works. There isn't a leading P&G brand anywhere that doesn't have a strong history of effective advertising."

Winning the World's Consumers

These simple principles are at the heart of P&G's success—and they're at work in every part of the P&G world.

"No matter where we're doing business, we stick to these principles," says Artzt. "Consumer needs may change from one country to another, but the way we understand and meet those needs doesn't change."

That's why we often reapply technologies, advertising and even consumer insights across geographies. We've built a world of leading brands by reapplying a world of ideas from people throughout Procter & Gamble.

On the following pages, highlights of a few of our brands demonstrate how P&G wins the trust and loyalty of the world's consumers—day after day, decade after decade.

Intent: The intent of this piece was to show shareholders why the company enjoys—and will continue to enjoy—great success.

Bottom Line: The bottom line of this piece is to:

- Highlight the reasons for P&G's success as a company
- Share the company's core principles
- Introduce the reader to the hard data that will follow in the annual report

The System in 10 Easy Steps

This particular piece served as the introduction to a Procter & Gamble annual report. It followed an opening letter by then-CEO Edwin Artzt and then-President John Pepper, which introduced the report by noting highlights of P&G's financial successes of the year. Following the section quoted above, P&G writers elaborated on each of its themes with examples: a section called "Winning with Breakthrough Technology" talked about how the company continues to perfect its Tide detergent. The next three sections, "Winning Consumers from the Start," "Winning with World-Class Advertising," and "Winning the World Over," all used similar examples of P&G products to make their points. The rest of the report analyzed the company's financial statements—a direct product of their work "Winning the World's Consumers."

Step 1: Questions and Research

1. **Who is my audience?** Procter & Gamble writers knew that the audience for this piece would be the company's shareholders.
2. **What do they want to know?** On the most fundamental level, shareholders always want to know how a company is doing. They also want insight into why the company succeeds (or fails) and how it plans to continue that success (or reverse any failure).
3. **What is my bottom line point?** In this case, the bottom line is that P&G succeeds because it builds brand loyalty among consumers.

Find out:

• How Procter & Gamble builds brand loyalty

Step 2: Evaluate Your Notes and Determine the Bottom Line

Instead of reviewing all the details that made up Procter & Gamble's piece here, take note of their theme—brand loyalty—and how they decided to focus on it. They took three pieces of the company's strategy to make their point: designing popular products by using technology to meet consumer needs, attracting first-time consumers, and using advertising to get customers' attention.

Step 3: Identify the Problem and Resolution

They said: The reader said:

Problem: P&G builds loyalty.   *Great—but how?*

Resolution: Our strategies help us win the world's consumers.

Fantastic! No wonder I bought your stock!

Step 4: Categorize Your Notes

Clearly, these writers had several categories to work with:

BRAND LOYALTY

TECHNOLOGICAL INNOVATION

WINNING FIRST-TIME CONSUMERS

ADVERTISING

USING PRINCIPLES TO SUCCEED WORLDWIDE

Step 5: Choose Development 3—Point of Insight

Of the categories above, the P&G writers chose ADVERTISING as their Point of Insight. They made that choice because without successful advertising, the best products disappear. Therefore:

They said:

Problem: P&G builds loyalty.

Development 1 (Background):

Development 2 (Bridge):

Development 3 (Point of Insight): Advertising builds loyalty.

Resolution: Our strategies help us win the world's consumers.

The reader said:

Great—but how?

It most definitely does!

Fantastic! No wonder I bought your stock!

Step 6: Choose Development 1—Background

Next, what background did P&G need to make its point effectively? The idea that technological innovation meets consumer needs in order to build the products its advertising will tout.

They said:

Problem: P&G builds loyalty.

Development 1 (Background):

   Technology meets consumer

   needs.

Development 2 (Bridge):

Development 3 (Point of

   Insight): Advertising builds

   loyalty.

Resolution: Our strategies help

   us win the world's consumers.

The reader said:

Great—but how?

Good strategy.

It most definitely does!

Fantastic! No wonder I bought

   your stock!

Step 7: Choose Development 2—Bridge

What's left? Getting consumers' attention the first time they enter the market:

They said:

Problem: P&G builds loyalty.

Development 1 (Background):

   Technology meets consumer

   needs.

Development 2 (Bridge): P&G

   targets first-time consumers.

The reader said:

Great—but how?

Good strategy.

Great idea!

Development 3 (Point of
   Insight): Advertising builds
   loyalty.

Resolution: Our strategies help
   us win the world's consumers.

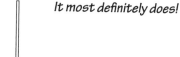

It most definitely does!

*Fantastic! No wonder I bought
your stock!*

Step 8: Create a List Outline—Organize Categories and Details

With the snapshot in place, let's take a look at what a List Outline for this piece might have looked like:

Problem: P&G builds loyalty.

Development 1 (Background): Technology meets consumer needs.

Development 2 (Bridge): P&G targets first-time consumers.

Development 3 (Point of Insight): Advertising builds loyalty.

Resolution: Our strategies help us win the world's consumers.

Quality and value build loyalty to Pampers, Ivory, etc.

Problem: P&G builds loyalty.

In every market P&G tries to understand consumer needs and keep up with them.
To do this consistently, the company requires "superior product technology."
This requires a sufficient breadth of product choices.
Technology allows P&G to offer products that meet a range of needs (Oil of Olay example).

Development 1 (Background): Technology meets consumer needs.

Another way to create loyalty: attract new consumers when they enter the prod-
uct category.
To do that, offer the right product at the right price.
Diaper example

Development 2 (Bridge): P&G targets first-time consumers.

"Advertising is the lifeblood of our brands"
VapoRub example
How advertising works—it tells consumers what the brand stands for.
It works—all leading brands have strong advertising history.

Development 3 (Point of Insight): Advertising builds loyalty.

Company sticks to these principles globally.
Consumer needs may change, but the way P&G understands them and tries to
meet them won't.
The company applies its three themes—technology, advertising, and consumer
insights—across geographies.
P&G has built a world of leading brands by reapplying a world of ideas from people throughout Procter & Gamble . . .

Resolution: Our strategies help us win the world's consumers.

Step 9: Add Transitions and an Opening Hook

The writers of this piece did a masterful job of keeping their theme—loyalty—
front and center throughout the piece in the transitions and in the opening hook.
If you look back at the finished piece, you'll see that the idea that the company
builds loyalty with its outstanding brands appears in every one of the report's
major transitions.

We see it first at the opening of Development 1. The Problem section, the piece's introduction, has just ended by making the point that to provide superior quality, the company continually adapts as consumer needs change. The next section opens with a quote from then-P&G President John Pepper: "In fact . . . the most important thing we do is to understand what consumers are looking for from a brand—and then consistently meet their needs with products of superior quality and value." The quote refers back to the idea of quality, looks forward with the mention of products, and talks about the theme—"what consumers are looking for from a brand."

In the same way, the end of the technology section both makes the point of that section and serves as a transition into the next: "Our commitment to these principles—delivering superior products that meet a range of consumer needs— is a key reason why consumers remain loyal to so many P&G brands."

The same goes for the opening of the third Development, which continues the thought "Our leading brands begin with world-class technology, but it's advertising that gets consumers' attention and persuades them to use our products again and again."

THE OPENING HOOK

This piece opens with a quote from then-CEO Ed Artzt, a good strategy especially when it comes to annual reports, which speak directly to the shareholder. Not only does this particular opening hook immediately address the theme of the piece—loyalty—it also humanizes it. In both opening hooks and transitions, quotes allow the person you are quoting to speak directly to the reader.

Step 10: Polish Your Draft

Procter & Gamble polished its annual report to a high sheen. It used headings to indicate the opening of each section and broke up paragraphs with white space and quotations. Most of all, notice that not a word of jargon or a pompous phrase made it into the final draft of this piece. The best writers never hide behind obtuse language, but use clear, everyday English.

Take one last look at the Procter & Gamble draft, this time with Target Outline elements in capitals and List Outline elements in bold and parentheses:

P&G BRANDS: WINNING THE WORLD'S CONSUMERS

(opening hook) "Everything we do is focused on building our brands," says P&G Chairman and Chief Executive Ed Artzt. That should come as no surprise, because Procter & Gamble is a company of brands—more than 300, in fact, marketed in over 140 countries. What makes P&G unique is not just the unparalleled number of leading brands our Company markets, but the enduring loyalty consumers have to our brands—across generations and geographies.

"Brand loyalty is the foundation of our business," Artzt says. "A new mother has to decide what brand of diapers to buy every week. Most consumers buy a box of laundry detergent 10 or 12 times a year. And every one of these purchase decisions is an opportunity to switch to another brand.

"But over the years, the consistent quality and value of our products have kept people coming back to Pampers, Ivory, Crest, Ariel and dozens of other P&G brands."

"We work hard to provide that superior quality and value day in and day out," says President John Pepper. "It means we must continually adapt to changing consumer needs."

PROBLEM: P&G BUILDS LOYALTY.

Understanding Consumer Needs (transition)

(major transition) "In fact," Pepper adds, "the most important thing we do is to understand what consumers are looking for from a brand—and then consistently meet their needs with products of superior quality and value." This is true in every market where our brands are sold, from the United States to the United Kingdom and from Mexico to China.

(transition) Artzt agrees. "Consumers have to trust that a brand will meet *all* their needs, all the time. That requires superior product technology. and it also requires a sufficient breadth of product choices. We should never give consumers a product reason to switch away from one of our brands."

(transition) Executive Vice President Durk Jager explains. "People can have a wide range of needs within a given category.

"A woman who uses Olay, for example, may need a face wash product first thing in the morning, a UV protectant during the day, and a replenishing cream at night. We make sure she can meet all those needs with one brand—Oil of Olay."

(major transition as well as bottom line of Development 1) Our commitment to these principles—delivering superior products that meet a range of consumer needs—is a key reason why consumers remain loyal to so many P&G brands.
DEVELOPMENT 1 (BACKGROUND): TECHNOLOGY MEETS CONSUMER NEEDS.

Creating Loyalty from the Start

(transition) Another way we create and build consumer loyalty is by attracting consumers the first time they purchase a product in one of our categories. "When new parents buy their first diapers, we want them to reach for Pampers," says Pepper.

To attract consumers at this "point of market entry," we must offer the right quality product at the right price.

(transition) "For example," says Pepper, "in some countries where incomes are low, striking this balance between quality and price requires us to market a diaper that offers more basic features, at a substantially lower price, than the premium diaper we sell in many countries."

(major transition as well as the bottom line of Development 2) The needs of consumers may vary from country to country, but the principle remains the same, as Artzt explains: "By winning consumer loyalty at this crucial decision point, we have the best opportunity to keep their loyalty for the long term." This focus on building consumer loyalty early is an important strategy for many P&G brands, including Always, Cover Girl and Clearasil.
DEVELOPMENT 2: P&G TARGETS FIRST-TIME CONSUMERS.

Building Loyalty with Advertising

(major transition) Our leading brands begin with world-class product technology, but it's advertising that gets consumers' attention and persuades them to use our products again and again.

"Advertising is the lifeblood of our brands," says Artzt, who points to Pantene Pro-V and Vicks VapoRub as recent examples of "products that became world brands on the strength of technology backed up by world-class advertising."

"We use advertising to tell consumers what our brands stand for," Jager adds. "And to show them why and how our brands will meet their needs. And we know it works. There isn't a leading P&G brand anywhere that doesn't have a strong history of effective advertising."

DEVELOPMENT 3 (POINT OF INSIGHT): ADVERTISING BUILDS LOYALTY.

Winning the World's Consumers

(major transition) These simple principles are at the heart of P&G's success—and they're at work in every part of the P&G world.

"No matter where we're doing business, we stick to these principles," says Artzt. "Consumer needs may change from one country to another, but the way we understand and meet those needs doesn't change."

(transition) That's why we often reapply technologies, advertising and even consumer insights across geographies. We've built a world of leading brands by reapplying a world of ideas from people throughout Procter & Gamble.

On the following pages, highlights of a few of our brands demonstrate how P&G wins the trust and loyalty of the world's consumers—day after day, decade after decade.

RESOLUTION: OUR STRATEGIES HELP US WIN THE WORLD'S CONSUMERS.

Part Three
Troubleshooting

In the first two parts of this book, you learned the system and watched it work in letters, reports, and proposals. Now it's time to try your own hand at writing. Before you do, though, this section provides some additional notes and a series of checklists to help you avoid detours along your path to the bottom line.

MORE ON TRANSITIONS AND OPENING HOOKS

Writing is all about making connections. You can't merely list facts; you've got to tie information and ideas together to make your reader understand whatever larger thought you hope to convey. That's why, beyond the level of basic structure, a piece of writing rises and falls on transitions and the opening hook. Walk your reader down a path. Don't drop him off a cliff, leave him standing alone in the wilderness, or fail to invite him on the trip at all.

Transitions

Transitions, as you've seen throughout this book, come in several forms. They signal changes in:

- Time. **Later, next, then, meanwhile, seven years ago . . .** All these words tell the reader we're moving forward or backward in time.
- Place. **On the other side of the street, in Italy, in our branch office, at headquarters, at the client site . . .** These tell the reader you're moving from one location to another.

- Concept. **Nevertheless, but, however, despite this, thus, therefore, given the above fact, on the other hand . . .** These signal a new idea coming, sometimes an idea that supports the previous one, sometimes an idea that takes the reader in a new direction.

If a reader is sufficiently well prepared for a change, you can use *invisible transitions*, which rely on formatting to signal a pause. Skip a line or use a heading and the reader knows to look for a new idea or section.

Repeated words can also serve as transitions. These transitions emphasize a point and, by creating a slight redundancy, make the reader focus on that idea as important. For example, in advertising copy: "We offer our customers service. When you call us, you'll get a person on the line, someone ready to help immediately. You won't be put on hold. Our standard of **service** is what has kept our company the lead auto repair shop in town for a quarter century . . .

In this case, the repeated word **service** highlights the theme and moves the reader from the opening paragraph to one about the company's long history in the local community.

Finally, there are *melding transitions*, those transitions that rely on a loaded word or phrase that connects two ideas. Some common melding words used in business writing include:

- **Investment,** as in "when you use our company, you're making an **investment** in quality." **Investment** ties the idea of payment to a perceived future benefit.
- **Classic,** as in "our product has lasted because it's a **classic**." **Classic** ties the idea of age to the idea of quality.
- **Share,** as in "Come to our café and we'll **share** our home cooking with you." **Share,** as a verb, connects the idea of offering a product to the concept of building a relationship.

- **Mansion, palace, castle,** as in "We turn any building into a **palace**." These words take the concept of a simple structure and add a connotation of size, beauty, and wealth to it.

Melding transitions work well to keep the theme of a proposal alive. For example, if your company's product is the oldest on the market, and you're trying to stress the company's experience and reliability, you might use a melding transition this way (highlighted in bold): "Your grandmother enjoyed Crunchy Oatmeal, so did your mother. Now you can use us, too. Since 1904, Crunchy Oatmeal has been serving customers all across the United States, and that's why we're known to generations." Transition: "We're still here because Crunchy Oatmeal is a **classic**. And **classics** endure. Today, with our new, improved features, Crunchy Oatmeal gives you that old-fashioned taste with modern convenience . . ."

Opening Hooks

Context opening hooks must simply orient the reader, providing enough information to lead him into the Problem. Ask yourself the traditional orientation questions: Who? What? Where? When? How? Why? to help orient your reader. You won't necessarily need to provide an immediate answer to every one of these questions, but they will help you get started.

Grabber opening hooks require creativity. To write a grabber opening, look through your notes for any unusual statistic, anecdote, or fact that you can *make relevant* to your problem. Putting ideas in concrete, human terms always serves better than offering broad generalizations. Look for ways to make your reader see and feel something. If you're writing a foundation's report on homelessness in your city, for example, using one individual's story personalizes the subject, while offering a startling statistic sheds light on the scope of the problem. Combining the two can sometimes offer the most powerful opening of all, for example:

> John Doe, originally from Iowa City, Iowa, came to Minneapolis with a good job as a construction foreman, several hundred dollars in savings, and high hopes for life in a new city. With no family to speak of, he thought Minneapolis offered a chance for a good future. He planned to settle here. But in 1993, just six months after moving, John got sick. A sudden heart attack left him weak and suffering from depression. It took months to work out disability payments, and even when he did, the money couldn't possibly cover all his expenses. After two years of unpaid bills, eviction, and debt, John Doe found himself living in shelters, moving nightly, looking for day work, sometimes spending a summer night in the park.
>
> There are nearly 6,000 people like John Doe in Minneapolis, sleeping every night under bridges and in doorways of a city that still thinks of itself as an old-fashioned community . . .

Grabber opening hooks help you give your reader a powerful boost, not only into the Problem, but into the whole piece. Beware, however, of using unrelated statistics or anecdotes merely for their dramatic appeal. No matter how strong, the opening hook only lends power to the piece as it relates to the overall theme. Using an unrelated or marginally related opening might get you immediate attention, but it will ultimately hurt you, because as soon as you try to make the jump into your *real* subject, your reader will become confused, disoriented, and ultimately uninterested.

THE SYSTEM IN 10 EASY STEPS

Step 1: Questions and Research

1. **Who is my audience?**
2. **What do they want to know?**
3. **What is my bottom line point?** Take notes, brainstorm, and research your topic to approach a bottom line.

Step 2: Evaluate Your Notes and Determine the Bottom Line

What do the details have in common? What conclusion can you draw from them? *What is the one big thing you want your reader to walk away knowing?*

Step 3: Identify the Problem and Resolution

Your Resolution should be a statement that makes your bottom line point, the single big idea you want to leave with the reader. Write a Problem statement that prompts the reader to ask a question for which the Resolution provides the answer.

Step 4: Categorize Your Notes

Categorize your notes to help you see the groups of ideas behind the details.

Step 5: Choose Development 3—Point of Insight

List your categories and decide which ones help the reader make the leap to the Resolution. What brings the reader that *aha!* moment? Label those categories D3 and write a statement that makes the reader say, "OH! If *that's* the case, there's no question *this* must be the Resolution!"

Step 6: Choose Development 1—Background

Decide which categories provide the necessary background your reader needs to understand your Resolution. Write a statement that expresses the point of that background.

Step 7: Choose Development 2—Bridge

What's left? Which category or categories logically build a bridge from your background to your point of insight? Label them, and write a bottom line that makes the point you need to bridge the gap in your ideas.

Step 8: Create a List Outline—Organize Categories and Details

Space out your Target Outline, leaving room *above* each statement. Organize your notes first by category and then by detail, so that ideas and facts flow logically to make the point of each outline statement.

Step 9: Add Transitions and an Opening Hook

Make connections both within outline "chunks" and after each outline statement, to introduce the new chunk. Open the document with a heading or sentence that orients the reader and draws him or her into your topic.

Step 10: Polish Your Draft

Smooth sentences, correct errors, and read your document aloud, looking for anything that will stop or confuse the reader. Format the document so it's easy on the eye.

THREE QUESTIONS AND CHOOSING A BOTTOM LINE

Common Mistakes and How to Correct Them

Mistake: You focus exclusively on what you want to say, forgetting what the reader wants to know.

If your reader wants to buy a car with better gas mileage, telling him how much cargo your model hauls won't help a bit. Storage might be an exciting feature you're anxious to tout, but if you fail to address the reader's need, he won't be listening.

Correction: Put anything you want to say in the context of what your reader needs. If you can *show* him he needs storage space in addition to—or even more than—mileage—great. If you can't, focus on what he's asked, not what you'd love to tell him.

Mistake: You base your bottom line on wishful thinking.

Your reader is the head of a beverage company who wants to know how the business can expand, and you think offering a new product—an energy drink—is the way to go. However, you do no research on the market or the consumer, so, although the market is already saturated with them, you propose a new sport drink targeted at young men, called Superwater.

Correction: Base your bottom line on research. Let the facts stimulate ideas.

THE TARGET OUTLINE

Common Mistakes and How to Correct Them

Mistake: Your Problem does not match your Resolution.

Problem: We can provide your company with the best security system on the market.	*(The reader asks: How?)*
Resolution: We offer you the lowest price.	*(The reader says: What does that have to do with it?)*

Correction: Before moving on to the rest of the Target Outline, look at the Problem and Resolution as a pair, without intervening details that can lead you astray. Make sure they ask, and answer, the same question.

Problem: We can provide your company with the best security system on the market.	*(The reader asks: How?)*
Resolution: Our experience and expertise show we can provide the best security system for your company.	*(The reader says: Oh, that's how!)*

Mistake: Your Development 3 is not a turning point. It does not provide the reader with a Point of Insight or, worse, it undercuts the Resolution.

Problem: I review Attila.	(The reader says: How did Attila perform this year?)
Development 3: Weakness requires improvement.	(The reader says: Does this guy really deserve a promotion?)
Resolution: Attila deserves a promotion.	(The reader says: I'm not sure about that!)

Correction: Test Development 3 by asking yourself the following question: What obvious conclusion must the reader jump to once he's read this?

Problem: I review Attila.	(The reader says: How did Attila perform this year?)
Development 3: Profit shows leadership.	(The reader says: He's ready to be a leader!)
Resolution: Attila deserves a promotion.	(The reader says: Yes, he does!)

Mistake: You choose irrelevant background for Development 1.

Problem: Brainstorm offers growth.	(The reader asks: How?)
Development 1: Our company has a long and hallowed history in the bottled water market.	(The reader says: Yes, I know, but what does that have to do with energy drinks?)
Resolution: Brainstorm will succeed because it serves a different kind of consumer.	(The reader says: It will? But we specialize in water!)

Correction: Choose background that moves your reader toward your Resolution.

Problem: Brainstorm offers growth.	*(The reader asks: How?)*
Development 1: Market bursts with	*(The reader says: Looks like a good*
potential.	*place to expand, but how do*
	we do it?)
Resolution: Brainstorm will succeed	*(The reader says: Oh, that's how!)*
because it serves a different kind	
of consumer.	

Mistake: Your Bridge does not connect D1 to D3 with a turning point idea.

Problem: Spendthrift faces risk.	*(The reader asks: How can I*
	protect myself?)
Development 1: Our methodology	*(The reader says: I can see that.*
yields reliable results.	*So what did you find?)*
Development 2: Spendthrift keeps	*(The reader says: I know that. So*
three separate accounts.	*what?)*
Development 3: Spendthrift risks fraud.	*(The reader says: Why? Is having*
	three accounts against the law
	now?)
Resolution: Spendthrift needs a system	*(The reader says: I'm a little*
to control its funds.	*confused.)*

Correction: Read your outline aloud and check that the logic flows.

Problem: Spendthrift faces risk.	*(The reader asks: How can I*
	protect myself?)
Development 1: Our methodology	*(The reader says: I can see that.*
yields reliable results.	*So what did you find?)*

Development 2: Findings reveal problems.	*(The reader says: I can see what I'm doing wrong. What are the consequences?)*
Development 3: Spendthrift risks fraud.	*(The reader says: I need help! What do I do?)*
Resolution: Spendthrift needs a system to control its funds.	*(The reader says: Sign me up!)*

Mistake: You decide an idea or fact is central because it's dramatic, rather than because it's pivotal.

In our Caesar proposal, the rebellion we put down in Galilee would make a great scene in a movie. However, Caesar hopes to avoid any public violence. While the information is important in our List Outline as one example of our experience handling any contingency, it's not what will most impress Caesar.

Be certain you construct your Target Outline based on the logic of what your audience is looking for, rather than on the emotional or dramatic power of a particularly flashy fact.

Correction: Evaluate the information using the question "What if?" What if we showed Caesar we could win a battle, but didn't show him we were able to be discreet? Would we still get the job? Not likely. On the other hand, what if we had never fought a public battle, but still showed that we could avoid one by poisoning all adversaries before open warfare became necessary? Caesar would probably hire us anyway.

THE LIST OUTLINE

Common Mistakes and How to Correct Them

Mistake: You've dumped your facts out like a laundry list, without giving them meaning.

Correction: Remember your reader. Ask yourself where the reader might get confused, or whether necessary information might have been left out, leaving him without context. Use your notes to make specific points, connect those points, and draw conclusions from them.

Mistake: Your notes, once assembled, don't support the Target Outline statements.

Correction: Return to the Target Outline. Your early research helped create that outline. If later research doesn't continue to support it, your ideas might simply be wrong. Evaluate all the facts, and, if necessary, rewrite your Target Outline.

If, on the other hand, your original conclusions are sound and the ideas that drive your Target Outline rest on real proof, you might have put that proof in the wrong place. Your facts are there, but disorganized. Review each chunk of the List Outline, and rearrange.

Mistake: You fail to organize your facts and ideas within the outline chunk so that each piece of information drives to the next, to make the point of the outline statement.

Correction: Approach the inside of each chunk in the same way you approach the Target Outline. Decide which information provides necessary context, which offers a point of insight, and what forms the bridge. Ask yourself if each sentence moves logically to the next and if the points you're making gain strength as they proceed.

POLISHING A DRAFT

Common Mistakes and How to Correct Them

Mistake: You're afraid to question yourself.

Correction: View every step in the Target Outline process as a place to test your logic. If at any time, for any reason, you find things not making sense, review each previous step. One advantage of breaking down the process is that it allows you to pinpoint errors and understand what went wrong—whether the mistake lies in your basic ideas, your organization of details, or simply at the level of how you expressed yourself.

Mistake: You get stuck on the opening hook.

Correction: You don't have to start drafting with the first sentence of your piece. Sometimes the pressure to begin at the beginning is too intense. Because all the pieces are already there in a well-developed List Outline, there's no reason the first polished sentence you write has to be the one at the very top. Move to a part of the outline where you're sure of yourself, where you have plenty of information to help you along, and begin there. Once you're comfortable putting any part of the outline into actual "language"—polished sentences and paragraphs—you'll usually be able to move up to the top and think of a good way to begin. If the hook still gives you trouble, stop trying so hard. Put down the most basic context necessary to orient the reader, and move on to express the point of your Problem. If you've gotten something down on paper—even if it's not much—it's easier to get creative with it.

Mistake: You get mired in polish.

Correction: Remember that ultimately, the ideas are what count. Polishing endlessly is only going to make you crazy.

Part Four
Exercises

Now it's time to try your hand at the system. The following exercises will help you hone your pre-writing skills by teaching you first to look for a bottom line and then to write your own. Next you'll practice each part of the Target Outline System, until you've written the entire draft of a full-length proposal. You can check your work against the Answer Key at the back of the book.

WHAT'S THE POINT?

Even if you're writing the most complicated technical report, you're still telling the reader a story. And that story can have one—and only one—overall message. Many details will no doubt make up that overall message, but at the end of the day, if you try telling your reader ten "big" things, he won't absorb even one.

The key to learning to find a bottom line is to learn the art of generalizing from small ideas to big ones. In the following exercises, practice ferreting out the bottom line in someone else's text, even when that person has not written in the most ideal, straightforward manner.

1.

Dear John,

I'm so sorry to have to let you go. The truth is, you've been a wonderful worker, and have shown tremendous loyalty to the company. Unfortunately, we've experienced a drop in revenue, and we're required to let the last person hired go first. I'd love to hire you back once times get better, but with the market the way it is, and customers spending less

on shoes, we just can't afford another salesman. Thanks again for your
hard work, and we'll give you your month's bonus as a sign of our ap-
preciation.
Thanks again for your hard work!
Amy

What's the point?

2.

In 2003, the U.S. Securities and Exchange Commission filed a complaint alleg-
ing that International Corporation had secretly paid the government of Guam to
help it sell more widgets. As a result, International Corp. formed a committee to
review ethics violations within the company and to make recommendations to
improve its practices. Those recommendations prompted International to estab-
lish Rule 304, which governs ethics in all aspects of its business.

What's the point?

3.

Dear Bill,
The issues involved in our recent project are complicated. For one, our
original deadline simply isn't realistic. Second, we've exceeded our

budget by fifteen percent, and an error in the original plan of service caused significant friction between the client and our subcontractor. Unrelated to that, two of the subcontractors on-site left during the third quarter. This obviously left us shorthanded, as it took us several weeks to recruit contractors with the requisite expertise. We lost another week soliciting Corporate for extra funds for them. In addition, the client has issued an addendum to its original plan, and Belinda has yet to incorporate that into our plan of service.

What's the point?

WRITE THE POINT

Each small list below boils down to a general bottom line. In this case, the audience is the CEO of Pennywise, a company that stocks dollar stores with low-cost trinkets, grooming accessories, and household tools. Read the notes for each paragraph. In the first two exercises, you'll be given a bottom line. Write the paragraph so it expresses that bottom line. In the last one, you'll need to deduce the bottom line on your own, then write the paragraph using the facts to express it.

1.

Notes:

- Pennywise Inc. faces a new rival, Poundfoolish Corp.
- Pennywise sells trinkets, household items, and grooming supplies to dollar stores.
- For ten years, Pennywise has dominated the regional market.
- Poundfoolish is a national company.

- Poundfoolish sells luxury items to department stores; it has now announced plans to move into the dollar store market.
- Poundfoolish plans to sell low-cost perfumes and hair accessories.
- Direct competition will be in hair accessories, which now make up Pennywise's bestselling category.

Bottom line: Pennywise faces a new threat, and must respond to it to protect its share of the market.

Paragraph:

2.

Notes:

- Poundfoolish motto: "luxury items at dollar store prices."
- Poundfoolish plans on using that motto to market directly to stores.
- Their theory—they can supply higher-end merchandise at competitive prices without many changes to their products.
- Theory remains untested.
- Can they sustain their product for dollar-store prices?

Bottom line: Poundfoolish's plan might fail.

Paragraph:

3.

Notes:

- Our products have a good reputation for quality.
- I recommend we shore up relationships with individual franchise-owners.
- I recommend we offer further discounts on hair products.
- If we remind store-owners we have a solid record with them, we'll be less likely to lose them.
- We can offer discounts on hair accessories, which remains our biggest seller.
- This could keep old business and bring in new.

Bottom line?
Paragraph:

KNOW YOUR READER

To write successfully, you've got to move out of your own point of view and think like your readers. What do they know, and what do they want to know? What information do they already have? Which facts will they find irrelevant, and which crucial? You'll always be writing from a body of facts, but choosing which ones to include and which to exclude depends on your target audience. In this exercise, you'll get to practice writing for different audiences, using the same basic facts. Use the scenario and notes provided to decide what to tell—and what not to tell—each of your audiences.

Scenario: It's December 1773, and you're one of the daring rebels who has just dumped British tea into Boston Harbor. You'll write a short account of what happened that night to three different audiences, drawing on the same set of facts:

You grew up in Boston, along with Sam Adams, a boyhood friend.

A patriot, you were furious when the British passed the Stamp Act in 1765. The act required colonists to buy and place stamps on all official documents, newspapers, pamphlets, and even playing cards.

In response, you joined Sam and his newly formed secret organization, the Sons of Liberty, in boycotts and protests designed to force the British to repeal the tax.

After some near-riots, the British did repeal the stamp tax in 1766, but followed in 1767 with the Townshend Acts, which taxed imports of glass, paint, paper, lead, and tea.

After two years of continued boycotts, Britain's new Prime Minister, Lord Frederick North, repealed most of the Townshend Acts, but left the tax on tea.

When you met Sam at your sister's wedding that same month, he reminded you that there are no half victories. The British kept the tax on tea to show they had the power to tax the colonies. Your battle cry remains "no taxation without representation."

By 1770, tensions in Boston had reached such a level that when an angry mob provoked some British soldiers, they shot into the crowd, killing five. You weren't there at the time, but it only hardened your resolve to resist British rule.

In 1773, the colonies got word of the Tea Act, a grant by Lord North to the East India Company to sell tea directly to the colonists, without the customs duty. The prime minister meant it to be a boon to the company, which was struggling financially. And it would have been. It meant the company could undercut American merchants, who sold smuggled Dutch tea. To add insult to injury, the East India tea would still be subject to the hated tea tax.

In every colony, patriots rejected the tax, and the tea that came with it. When the East India Company's ships tried to land, they were turned away in New York and Philadelphia. In Charleston, the ships landed, but colonists put the tea into government warehouses and left it to rot.

Here in Boston, three ships arrived, allowed in by the loyalist governor, Thomas Hutchinson, a personal enemy of Sam's. The ships sat at Griffin's Wharf, surrounded by armed British warships.

Hundreds of patriots gathered on the docks, refusing to let the company unload its tea. Still, Hutchinson refused to let it leave port.

Commanders of the armed ships announced that if the rebels would not allow the tea to be unloaded by December 17, they would force it onto shore under cannon cover.

On the 16th, you met in church with fellow Bostonians to discuss the crisis. Though you favored immediately storming the ships, others wanted to give Hutchinson a chance to back down. All agreed to dispatch a committee to petition the governor for satisfaction.

Hutchinson told the committee he would deliver his answer at five o'clock that evening, but when the men returned at five to see him, he'd gone on an errand six miles away.

You weren't at all surprised, as you'd known him in younger years, and he'd always been a coward. With no response from Hutchinson, the meeting dissolved, and the Sons of Liberty knew their duty, which they'd discussed for several days as the debate raged.

That night, you dressed as a Mohawk Indian, armed yourself with a small hatchet, and met others in the street as you headed to Griffin's Wharf.

There, men split into three groups and boarded the ships. The soldiers on the armed ships stood by without reacting, while you demanded the keys to the hatches and candles, with which to find the tea.

When the captain surrendered these, you removed the chests of tea, broke them open with hatchets, and threw them overboard.

One or two Bostonians tried to sneak aboard to pocket some tea for home use, but they were set upon, kicked, and sent on their way. One ended up in the water with the tea.

The next morning, tea still floated on Boston Harbor, and you took small boats to beat it down with oars, so it would be too drenched to use.

Write a paragraph or two using any or all of these facts to each of the audiences listed below:

1. Future Americans, for whom you want to write a formal history of the event
2. Your brother James, now in school in Philadelphia
3. Your leader, Samuel Adams, who has asked for a report of the night's adventure

(Compare your paragraphs to those in the Answer Key.)

HIGH-LEVEL POLISH— ESTABLISHING THE RIGHT TONE

In Exercise 3, you were given a set of facts and asked to write to three different audiences: future Americans, your brother James, and Sam Adams, your leader. In this exercise, use the paragraphs you wrote there, but polish them for tone. That means using the appropriate language and style for the audience.

1.

When writing a formal history, keep your distance from the reader. You are meant to come across as all-knowing, so don't equivocate. Set down the facts, avoid personal asides, and keep your language clear and proper. Use the third person, avoiding "I" and "you."

Write a paragraph using the same facts you used before, but with the formal tone required:

2.

When writing to your brother, feel free to use colloquial language, to make jokes, and to be creative with sentence structure. Write in the first person, using "I."

Write a paragraph using the same facts you used earlier, but with the informal tone required:

3.

When writing to your superior, you may write in the first person and address him directly, but avoid slang, don't be too personal, and keep your language formal.

Write a paragraph using the same facts as before, but with the correct tone:

WRITING A GRABBER OPENING HOOK

You've been assigned to write a report on theme parks for a company hoping to open a small, indoor amusement park. Your Target Outline appears below. Using the point of the Problem statement and the facts provided, write a grabber opening hook for your report.

You say:	The reader says:
Problem: Theme parks require unifying vision, consistent maintenance, and strong management.	What does each involve?
Development 1 (Background): Theme defines rides, games, and food areas.	I understand.
Development 2 (Bridge): Parks require regular maintenance	I can see the importance of that.
Development 3 (Point of Insight): Management keeps park running.	That's the most important element!
Resolution: Parks require vision, maintenance, and management.	I can see that!

Facts:

North America boasts nearly 600 theme parks, including outdoor amusement parks and water parks.

The first U.S. amusement park was Steeplechase Park at Coney Island in Brooklyn, New York, which opened in 1897.

There are 634 roller coasters in the United States.

An estimated 175 million people visited America's fifty most popular amusement parks in 2005.

ELIMINATING JARGON

Jargon can be any of the following:

- Highly specialized words that replace simple English
- Verbs turned into noun phrases (Investigate becomes "perform an investigation.")
- Nouns turned into nonexistent verbs ("Incentive" becomes "incentivize.")
- Excessive wordiness—to the point that the reader has to wade through so many extra words he loses track of your meaning

Circle the examples of jargon and excessive wordiness found in the statements and paragraphs that follow. If possible, translate into English:

1. My suggestion is that we create a metric to determine the rate of response to our most recent poll.
2. The idea suggested by you does not in any way conform to the policy-set we have established as the norm here at Data Center.
3. Anticipating early precipitation, the superannuated agrarian collected his canines, several of which were contumacious in their resistance to

reentering the structure housing cattle. After several attempts at affrighting the unmannerly quadrupeds, he made the decision to primarily shelter himself, and abandoned them.

4. A study should be conducted to determine which routes present the highest potential profit-margin. Once it is ascertained which routes present the most lucrative prospects, Grand Airlines could and should expand its air service in such a way as to take advantage of said routes.

5. Internet World is focused on stimulation of ideation, and it is for that purpose that we incentivize employees with encouragement of submissions of their unique idea-sets centered on ways to better improve our corporate setting.

6. Facilitation of an on-time filing of taxable income information required by the IRS is the impetus behind the Zelmar Corporation CFO's decision to stagger the company's review of financial data, which, in the previous annum, caused Zelmar to incur a financial penalty mandated by law in the amount of $20,000 as a direct result of post-due filing. This annum, to facilitate the filing ASAP, Zelmar's CFO has instituted an early-report deadline, to be received 30 days prior to the IRS filing due date.

FORMATTING

Format the following data, using bullets, headings, and white space to make it more readable:

The leading causes of occupational injury deaths were motor-vehicle-related injuries (33%), injuries caused by machines (16%), shootings (11%), falls (10%), electrical accidents (6%), and incidents during which a worker was hit by a falling object (4%).

The mining industry suffered the highest average annual fatality rates (32.9 per 100,000 workers), followed by construction (24.6), transportation/communication/public utilities (23.3), and agriculture/forestry/fishing (17.3).

WRITING A PROPOSAL

Imagine that before the Boston Tea Party, Samuel Adams asks you to write a proposal on how best to force the British to stop their campaign of taxation. He is looking for ways to cause them enough pain so they'll rethink their attitude toward the colonists. Create a proposal that tells Adams exactly what you plan to do and how it will hurt the British. Make sure you include relevant background, possible problems you might encounter, and benefits to the colonists if the project succeeds.

Using the Target Outline system, walk through the ten steps. In this extended final exercise, you'll not only write a Target and List Outline, you'll also evaluate your List Outline and do directed research to fill in gaps.

Step 1: Questions and Research

Ask yourself:

1. **Who is my audience?**
2. **What does he want to know?**
3. **What is my bottom line point?**

Use the following notes to help you decide on your bottom line:

The British have been provoking us for eight years, since the Stamp Act. Each time, we boycott and they repeal some or all of the taxes. But they always try again.

We boycotted stamps, we boycotted the Townshend duties, and yet the tax on tea remains.

Our battle cry, as you've often said, is "no taxation without representation" and this is an awful case of it.

Lord North thinks he can trick us into accepting taxes on imports, like tea, but we won't accept it.

We owe the British a big response after they killed five colonists in 1770.

Philadelphia and New York turned the ships away, Charleston left the tea to rot in a warehouse, but here, Hutchinson insists the ships remain and wants us to pay the duty. We must respond in a dramatic way.

At Griffin's Wharf, three British ships sit. They're surrounded by armed ships of war.

Commanders of the armed ships say that if we don't allow the tea to be unloaded by December 17, they will force it onto shore under cannon cover.

These ships present an opportunity to force the Crown to recognize our rights as citizens. We lost much when Hutchinson allowed the ships to dock. If we don't act, the British will see Boston as a weak link in the resistance movement.

Hutchinson has also challenged us by insisting he won't let the ships leave unless we pay the duty. He's trying to break us.

If we allow the East India Company to gain even a small foothold in Boston, they'll never let go. They need the money and won't hesitate to use force once they see some of our people will buy their tea.

Therefore, we can't allow any of the tea to reach Boston. Loyalists will
create a market for it, and undercut the whole revolutionary move-
ment.

I believe we ought to destroy the cargo.

We can dress as Mohawk Indians, disguise our faces with coal dust,
and carry hatchets to use on the trunks of tea.

We can divide into three groups, each led by one man. One man should
be assigned to approach the ship's captain and demand candles
and the keys to the hold where the tea sits.

We should prepare some of our number to respond in case the soldiers
on the surrounding ships react.

We should use our hatchets to break open the chests and make sure the
water can reach all the tea.

Once we've opened them all, we'll dump them into the harbor.

The East India Company nearly bankrupted itself trying to expand
trade into India. The loss of so much tea could ruin it.

Causing such a loss to the Company would be a direct slap to Lord
North, who hopes to trick us into accepting taxation by selling us
cheap tea.

It would also be a rebuke to Governor Hutchinson, who is not only a
loyalist, but whose sons stand to gain from the tea sales as employ-
ees of the East India Company.

The East India Company announced plans to bring in its own agents to
sell tea here in the colonies. This would hurt American merchants,
cutting them out of the tea business altogether.

Step 2: Evaluate Your Notes and Fill in the Bottom Line

Imagine your bottom line is the losses Britain and its allies will suffer if your plan for the Boston Tea Party succeeds. What question do you want Sam Adams asking when he reads the opening of your proposal? What question will drive him to look for your Resolution? Fill in the Problem and Resolution statements below, as well as what it should prompt the reader to say.

Step 3: Identify the Problem and Resolution

You say:

The reader says:

Problem:

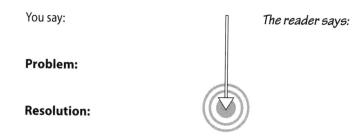

Resolution:

Check your statements to make sure they match. Does the Resolution answer the question raised by the Problem? Have you satisfied the reader's curiosity?

Step 4: Categorize Your Notes

Look back at the notes at the beginning of this exercise. Categorize them so that you can choose the turning point ideas that will make up your three Developments. (If you get stuck, check the Answer Key.)

Step 5: Choose Development 3—Point of Insight

You now have a half-filled Target Outline and a list of categories for your notes. Imagine what follows are your Problem and Resolution and note categories. What facts or ideas will make your reader see that your Resolution will work?

You say:		The reader says:
Problem: We must cause the British pain so they'll stop taxing us.		*Yes, but how?*
Development 1 (Background):		
Development 2 (Bridge):		
Development 3 (Point of Insight):		
Resolution: Dumping the tea will hurt our enemies.		*Brilliant!*

Categories of Notes:

PROVOCATION
WHAT'S AT STAKE
PLAN
BENEFITS

What category belongs in Development 3?
Write an outline statement to reflect your point for that Development.

Step 6: Choose Development 1—Background

Your outline now looks this way:

You say:		The reader says:
Problem: We must cause the British pain so they'll stop taxing us.		*Yes, but how?*

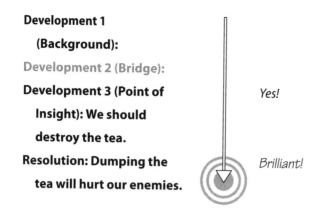

**Development 1
   (Background):**
Development 2 (Bridge):
**Development 3 (Point of
   Insight): We should
   destroy the tea.**

Yes!

**Resolution: Dumping the
   tea will hurt our enemies.**

Brilliant!

What background does Sam Adams need to help persuade him that your plan is the way to go?

What category belongs in Development 1?

Write an outline statement to reflect your point for that Development.

Step 7: Choose Development 2—Bridge

Your outline now looks this way:

You say:

**Problem: We must cause the
   British pain so they'll stop
   taxing us.**

**Development 1 (Background):
   Provocation demands
   dramatic response.**

**Development 2
   (Bridge):**

The reader says:
Yes, but how?

I can see your point.

Development 3 (Point of Insight): We should destroy the tea.

Yes!

Resolution: Dumping the tea will hurt our enemies.

Brilliant!

What point connects your background—that British provocation demands a dramatic response—to your Point of Insight—that destroying the tea should *be* that dramatic response?

What category belongs in Development 2?

Write an outline statement to reflect your point for that Development.

Step 8, Part 1: Create a List Outline—Organize Categories and Details

You now have a complete Target Outline:

You say:

Problem: We must cause the British pain so they'll stop taxing us.

The reader says:

Yes, but how?

Development 1 (Background): Provocation demands dramatic response.

I can see your point.

Development 2 (Bridge): They stand to lose if we do this; we stand to lose if we don't.

The stakes are high!

Development 3 (Point of Insight): We should destroy the tea.

Yes!

Resolution: Dumping the tea will hurt our enemies.

Brilliant!

You also have a list of notes and categories:

PROVOCATION
WHAT'S AT STAKE
PLAN
BENEFITS

Use the graphic that follows to turn the Target Outline into a List Outline. Put the categories of notes where they belong, and try to decide where to put categories you've not yet labeled.

Problem: We must cause the British pain so they'll stop taxing us.

Development 1 (Background): Provocation demands dramatic response.

Development 2 (Bridge): They stand to lose if we do this; we stand to lose if we don't.

Development 3 (Point of Insight): We should destroy the tea.

Resolution: Dumping the tea will hurt our enemies.

Problem: We must cause the British pain so they'll stop taxing us.

Development 1 (Background): Provocation demands dramatic response.

```
┌─────────────────────────────────────────────────┐
│                                                 │
└─────────────────────────────────────────────────┘
                        ▼
```

Development 2 (Bridge): They stand to lose if we do this; we stand to lose if we don't.

```
┌─────────────────────────────────────────────────┐
│                                                 │
└─────────────────────────────────────────────────┘
                        ▼
```

Development 3 (Point of Insight): We should destroy the tea.

```
┌─────────────────────────────────────────────────┐
│                                                 │
└─────────────────────────────────────────────────┘
                        ▼
```

Resolution: Dumping the tea will hurt our enemies.

Step 8, Part 2: Evaluate Your List Outline

Look below at your current List Outline, with notes substituted for the categories that helped you do your initial organizing. Examine the outline for any breaks in logic, missed connections, or weaknesses in your research. Remember that the outline statements represent the culmination of the notes above them. Evaluate those notes to be certain they make the point of each statement.

Problem: We must cause the British pain so they'll stop taxing us.

Development 1 (Background): Provocation demands dramatic response.

Development 2 (Bridge): They stand to lose if we do this; we stand to lose if we don't.

Development 3 (Point of Insight): We should destroy the tea.

Resolution: Dumping the tea will hurt our enemies.

This proposal addresses the tea problem we've been discussing. Given the situation, we have no choice but to respond to this latest provocation in a way that causes the British real pain, so they will stop taxing us once and for all.

Problem: We must cause the British pain so they'll stop taxing us.

The British have been provoking us for eight years, since the Stamp Act. Each time, we boycott and they repeal some or all of the taxes. But they always try again. **PROVOCATION**

We boycotted stamps, we boycotted the Townshend duties, and yet the tax on tea remains. **PROVOCATION**

Our battle cry, as you've often said, is "no taxation without representation" and this is an awful case of it. **PROVOCATION**

Lord North thinks he can trick us into accepting taxes on imports, like tea, but we won't accept it. **PROVOCATION**

We owe the British a big response after they killed five colonists in 1770. **PROVOCATION**

Philadelphia and New York turned the ships away, Charleston left the tea to rot in a warehouse, but here, Hutchinson insists the ships remain and wants us to pay the duty. We must respond in a dramatic way. **PROVOCATION**

At Griffin's Wharf, three British ships sit. They're surrounded by armed ships of war. **PROVOCATION**

Commanders of the armed ships say that if we don't allow the tea to be unloaded by December 17, they will force it onto shore under cannon cover. **PROVOCATION**

The East India Company announced plans to bring in its own agents to sell tea here in the colonies. This would hurt American merchants, cutting them out of the tea business altogether. **PROVOCATION**

Development 1 (Background): Provocation demands dramatic response.

These ships present an opportunity to force the Crown to recognize our rights as citizens. We lost much when Hutchinson allowed the ship to dock. If we don't act, the British will see Boston as a weak link in the resistance movement. **WHAT'S AT STAKE**

Hutchinson has also challenged us, by insisting he won't let the ships leave unless we pay the duty. He's trying to break us. **WHAT'S AT STAKE**

If we allow the East India Company to gain even a small foothold in Boston, they'll never let go. They need the money, and won't hesitate to use force once they see some of our people will buy their tea. **WHAT'S AT STAKE**

Therefore, we can't allow any of the tea to reach Boston. Loyalists will create a market for it and undercut the whole revolutionary movement. **WHAT'S AT STAKE**

**Development 2 (Bridge): They stand to lose if we do this;
we stand to se if we don't.**

I believe we ought to destroy the cargo. **PLAN**

We can dress as Mohawk Indians, disguise our faces with coal dust, and carry hatchets to use on the trunks of tea. **PLAN**

We can divide into three groups, each led by one man. One man should be assigned to approach the ship's captain and demand candles and the keys to the hold where the tea sits. **PLAN**

We should prepare some of our number to respond, in case the soldiers on the surrounding ships react. **PLAN**

We should use our hatchets to break open the chests and make sure the water can reach all the tea. **PLAN**

Once we've opened them all, we should dump them into the harbor. **PLAN**

Development 3 (Point of Insight): We should destroy the tea.

> The East India Company nearly bankrupted itself trying to expand trade into India. The loss of so much tea could ruin it. **BENEFITS**
>
> Causing such a loss to the Company would be a direct slap to Lord North, who hopes to trick us into accepting taxation by selling us cheap tea. **BENEFITS**
>
> It would also be a rebuke to Governor Hutchinson, who is not only a loyalist, but whose sons stand to gain from the tea sales as employees of the East India Company. **BENEFITS**

Resolution: Dumping the tea will hurt our enemies.

Evaluate the notes above with the following questions:

1. Do the notes within each chunk make the outline statement's point?
2. Are the notes within each chunk organized logically? Do they move from one point to the next, gaining power with each new addition?
3. Is the strongest point in each of the chunks at the end, nearest the outline statement?
4. Is any important information missing?

Step 8, Part 3: Do Directed Research

Our last exercise showed us that we have a hole in our outline. The Resolution would be stronger if we quantified what the East India Company stands to lose if we succeed. We now have two research questions:

How much tea do these ships carry?

How much would be lost if we actually dumped the tea into the sea?

At this stage in the outlining system, you'll do directed research to find the answers. Read the documents that appear on the next several pages. Don't, however, read looking for just anything. Directed research means reading with the high beams on—searching only for the specific answers to your questions. Keep those questions in mind, and try reading through the information quickly, skimming the first sentence of each paragraph to assess whether your answer might be there. If not, skip to the next paragraph. Once you find what you're looking for, slow down and read carefully. Remember that this is unlike preliminary research, where you read with an open mind, assessing everything to see what point you want to make. Here you are simply searching for one or two pinpointed pieces of information. Don't be led astray by interesting but irrelevant new facts.

Document 1

The Sons of Liberty obtained the following letter, written by a representative of the East India Company to his superiors in England:

Dear Sir,

I write you with great excitement. The colonies, as promised, present an excellent new market for us. Soon, all our difficulties should be solved. Though the Company finds itself in great debt, His Majesty's recent boon seems likely to restore our fortunes.

The colonists are certain to make a fuss when they discover we will be sending our own agents. However, any protest ought to die down soon enough. I fear reports of American unruliness have made some of my colleagues uneasy, but on my honour, sir, they have been greatly exaggerated. A few unruly boys hurl stones, British soldiers return fire, and they call it a massacre! Even the colonists' own John Adams sided with our men. He represented them here in court, most were acquitted, and there's been nary a response. And to think Randolph Owens predicted a riot!

As to the business at hand, you asked what shipment I would suggest. As the people here drink great amounts of smuggled Dutch tea, sold at higher price, I urge you to send the full shipment. Fill the holds full of tea, and hurry them here. We stand to make a great profit!

Your faithful servant,

Joseph Dalrymple

Document 2

Your friend Josiah Shaw, a dockworker, passed you this manifest:

Manifest of the Good Ship *Dartmouth*
November 1773

Crew:

Fourteen souls, employees of the British East India Company:

Captain, Francis Rotch	White Leggett
First mate, Jacob Smithe	William Button
Ship's doctor, apothecary, Matthew Grady	Edward Doty
Ship's cook, Solomon Peterson	Thomas English
John Alden	Moses Fletcher
Isaac Allerton	John Holbeck
Bartholomew Carter	Richard Hooke

Cargo:

20 bolts Indian silk

12 trunks paper

13 trunks lead, green and red

100 pounds chocolate

342 chests tea

200 chests sugar

Signed this 3rd day of November 1773,

By Francis Rotch, Master of the ship *Dartmouth*

Document 3

Patriots in New York sent you this newspaper report from the *New York Gazette* of tea turned away from their dock:

On Tuesday morning, three ships of the British East India Company attempted to dock at New York Harbor, to deliver the tea sent under the Tea Act. Fifty resolute patriots rowed out to meet them armed with muskets, and threatened violence if the ships approached shore.

The Company men had only to look to land, where a thousand citizens of New York were gathered, to see the trouble that awaited if they dared continue their approach. As such, observers watching the decks noted frantic activity for the better part of an hour as the captains of the three ships congregated on the lead vessel to confer.

Negotiations ensued, as the loss facing the East India Company was great. The ships, together carrying tea worth some 10,000 pounds sterling, would suffer the loss, not just of the tea sale, but of the other goods on board, notably paper, silk, sugar and lead.

The captain of the lead ship argued that he should be allowed to dock and unload all but the tea, as the other goods were no longer subject to the Townshend Duty. However, suspecting a trick, the patriots refused, and several more boatloads of young men sailed to bolster their fellows.

Upon seeing this, the captain retreated, and the ships turned seaward, never having reached port.

Step 9, Part 1: Add Transitions

You've organized each chunk of the List Outline and filled in holes with additional research. Now add transitions. Write the following transitions:

1. At the end of the Problem section, imagine you had written "If we can provide a painful consequence to the British in response to this latest provocation, we might deter them from taxing us again."

Write a transition that will take you from that statement into the beginning of Development 1. Don't worry about using colonial-style language. Write the transition as if you were speaking to your manager or boss today. Remember, the point of the Background chunk will be that British provocation requires a dramatic response.

Your transition:

2. At the end of Development 1, imagine you've made your point by writing: "In Philadelphia and New York, colonists succeeded in turning the ships back. In Charleston they accepted shipment, but left it to rot in the warehouses. Here in Boston we can do no less. Boycott is no longer enough; we must take dramatic action."

Write a transition that will take you from that statement into the beginning of Development 2. The point of the Bridge Development will be that your enemies stand to lose much if you act; you stand to lose if you don't.

Your transition:

3. Development 2 might close by referring to Governor Hutchinson's challenge to the Sons of Liberty: "We have no choice but to answer it. If we do, the advantages will be great, as we can strike a blow at the British, Hutchinson, and the East India Company at once."

Write a transition that moves from that thought into Development 3, the section in which you lay out your plan for the Boston Tea Party.

Your transition:

4. Write a transition into your Resolution, which will sum up the benefits of the plan. Try to make this transition complex—make sure it not only moves your reader into the new section, but reminds him of the overall point of your proposal.

Your transition:

Step 9, Part 2: Write an Opening Hook

Write an opening hook for your Boston Tea Party proposal.

Step 10: Polish Your Draft

All the elements of your draft should be in place. Now polish and format your proposal so that it reads smoothly, is free of error, and has the proper headings and spacing.

Answer Key

Exercise 1: What's the Point?

1. Amy's being nice, but the bottom line remains the cold, hard truth: John, you're fired.
2. Although the history of bribery is flashy, it's mainly there to help you understand the bottom line: Rule 304 sets the ethical standard for International Corporation.
3. This is a tricky one, as the writer is all over the map when it comes to complaining about how complicated his issues are. However, the preponderance of the information points to one bottom line: This project won't meet its deadline.

Exercise 2: Write the Point

Though your wording might differ from what follows, the paragraphs on the next page each express a bottom line based on the facts. Compare them to yours to see if you did the same:

1. For ten years, Pennywise has dominated the regional market for supplying dollar stores with trinkets, household tools, and hair supplies. We now face a new rival: the national Poundfoolish. Although Poundfoolish has traditionally targeted department stores, it recently announced plans to move into the dollar store market with a line of low-cost perfumes and hair accessories. As you know, hair accessories are our company's best sellers. To prevent losses in this category, Pennywise needs a plan to compete against Poundfoolish's new product line and protect our market share.

Bottom line: Pennywise faces a new threat and must respond to it to protect its share of the market.

2. Poundfoolish plans to use its motto "luxury items at dollar store prices" to market directly to stores. Their untested theory is that they can supply higher-end merchandise at competitive prices by making few changes to their products. There remains some doubt as to whether they will be able to sustain the quality of their products for dollar store prices.

Bottom line: Poundfoolish's plan might fail.

3. I recommend we respond in two ways: by shoring up relationships with individual franchise owners and by offering further discounts on hair products. Our products have always had a reputation for quality, and by reminding store-owners of our excellent track record with them, we will be less likely to lose them to Poundfoolish. In addition, if we offer a discount on hair accessories, which remain our biggest sellers, we are likely to keep customers we already supply and possibly draw new business.

Bottom line: Two-pronged plan could help us fight Poundfoolish.

Exercise 3: Know Your Reader

1. To write a formal history, you will need to include lots of background. Assume your reader knows nothing about the events leading up to the

Boston Tea Party. Explain the Stamp Act, the Townshend Act, and the Tea Act. Include information on the East India Company and on the major players—Samuel Adams, Thomas Hutchinson, Lord North. Since this is a formal history, leave out personal asides. The reader doesn't need to know that you met Sam at your sister's wedding and discussed the tea tax, or that you know that Thomas Hutchinson has always been a coward.

2. Your brother James already knows all about the Stamp Act and all the other British provocations. He's well aware of colonial history up until December 16. He wants to hear what happened that day—and he wants every detail, including the aside that Tom Hutchinson ran from the colonists.

3. Sam Adams requires a formal report, but he also knows all the history that led up to the Boston Tea Party. He does not want personal asides or opinions, nor does he need to be reminded of the events of the meeting that led to the decision to raid the ships. He wants only the facts he missed—what happened on the ship you boarded, how the operation went, and what problems, if any, you encountered.

Exercise 4: High-Level Polish—Establishing the Right Tone

1. Your formal history might sound something like this:

The Stamp Act of 1765 required colonists to buy and place British revenue stamps on all official documents, including correspondence, newspapers, pamphlets, and playing cards. The colonists refused to buy the stamps, and their protests sometimes turned violent. In 1766, hoping to calm tensions, the British government repealed the tax. Peace did not last long, however. In 1767, Lord Frederick North, Britain's new prime minister, imposed the Townshend Duties on imports of glass, paper, paint, lead, and tea.

2. Your personal letter might sound this way:

That Hutchinson! He was as much a coward as ever, and, James, you know that's saying something. Those two spoiled sons of his were made agents of the East India Company, of all things—you can imagine what that means. Hutchinson insisted the tea would sit at Griffin's Wharf until we paid. But we showed them! Sam Adams and some of the others you'd remember planned a surprise for old Hutchinson, and those lobsterbacks threatening to unload the tea under cannon cover. I wish you could have been there!

3. Your note to Sam Adams could read:

As you requested, I've detailed the events of what's now being called our "Tea Party." The operation proceeded smoothly once the church meeting had dissolved. As you directed, the men disguised themselves with coal dust and proceeded in three groups of fifty to Griffin's Wharf. There, one man was dispatched to each ship to demand the captain point out the holds that contained the tea and provide candles so we could see.

Exercise 5: Writing a Grabber Opening Hook

All the facts provided are interesting, and with some creativity, almost any could be used. But the one that most easily drives toward the point of your Problem statement is the last one—that 175 million people visited America's fifty most popular amusement parks in 2005. Your grabber opening could sound something like this:

In 2005, an estimated 175 million people visited America's most popular amusement parks. With more than the population of some countries attending theme parks each year, running a theme park requires a unifying vision, consistent maintenance, and most of all, solid management.

Exercise 6: Eliminating Jargon

1. My suggestion <u>is that</u> we <u>create a metric</u> to determine the <u>rate of response</u> to our most recent poll.

    Translation: I suggest we measure how quickly people respond to our poll.

2. The idea <u>suggested by you</u> does not <u>in any way conform</u> to the <u>policy-set</u> we have established <u>as the norm</u> here at Data Center.

    Translation: That is against our policy.

3. Anticipating early <u>precipitation</u>, the <u>superannuated agrarian</u> collected his <u>canines</u>, several of which were <u>contumacious</u> in their resistance to reentering the <u>structure housing cattle</u>. After several attempts at <u>affrighting</u> the <u>unmannerly quadrupeds</u>, he made the decision to <u>primarily</u> shelter himself, and abandoned them.

    Translation: Anticipating early rain, the old farmer collected his dogs, several of which stubbornly refused to enter the barn. He tried a few times to frighten them, then decided to get out of the rain himself, and left them there.

4. <u>A study should be conducted</u> to determine which routes present the <u>highest potential profit-margin</u>. Once <u>it is ascertained</u> which routes present the most <u>lucrative prospects</u>, Grand Airlines <u>could and should</u> expand its air service <u>in such a way as to</u> take advantage of <u>said</u> routes.

    Translation: Grand Airlines should study which routes would be most lucrative, then expand air service accordingly.

5. Internet World <u>is focused on stimulation of ideation</u>, and <u>it is for that purpose</u> that we <u>incentivize</u> employees <u>with encouragement of submissions of their unique idea-sets centered on ways</u> to <u>better improve</u> our corporate <u>setting</u>.

    Translation: At Internet World we welcome suggestions.

6. Facilitation of an on-time filing of taxable income information required by the IRS is the impetus behind the Zelmar Corporation CFO's decision to stagger the company's review of financial data, which, in the previous annum, caused Zelmar to incur a financial penalty mandated by law in the amount of $20,000 as a direct result of post-due filing. This annum, to facilitate the filing ASAP, Zelmar's CFO has instituted an early-report deadline, to be received 30 days prior to the IRS filing due date.

Translation: Last year's financial review delayed Zelmar Corporation's tax filing. As a result, it paid $20,000 in penalties. This year, the company's chief financial officer has decided to stagger the review, with the final report due 30 days before the filing deadline.

Exercise 7: Formatting

The leading causes of occupational injury deaths were:

- Motor-vehicle related injuries (33%)
- Injuries caused by machines (16%)
- Shootings (11%)
- Falls (10%)
- Electrical accidents (6%)
- Incidents during which a worker was struck by a falling object (4%)

The industrial sectors with the highest average annual fatality rates were:

- Mining (32.9 per 100,000 workers)
- Construction (24.6)
- Transportation/communication/public utilities (23.3)
- Agriculture/forestry/fishing (17.3)

Exercise 8: Writing a Proposal

STEP 1: QUESTIONS AND RESEARCH

1. **Who is my audience?** Sam Adams
2. **What does he want to know?** How can we deliver a real blow to our enemies?
3. **What is my bottom line point?** (see below)

STEP 2: EVALUATE YOUR NOTES AND DETERMINE THE BOTTOM LINE

The bottom line point here is the loss that the British, and everyone else who supports the taxation, will sustain if our plan succeeds.

STEP 3: IDENTIFY THE PROBLEM AND RESOLUTION

Although you can word this Problem and Resolution pair in several ways, they must essentially say the following:

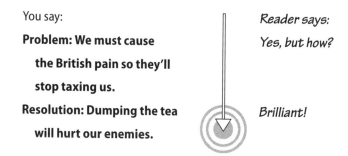

You say:

Problem: We must cause the British pain so they'll stop taxing us.

Resolution: Dumping the tea will hurt our enemies.

Reader says:

Yes, but how?

Brilliant!

The reader's question here has to do with how to cause the British enough pain to discourage taxation. Use the "what if" question to find out what the Resolution ought to be. What if the colonists dumped tea into the harbor, but the East India Company was rich enough to absorb the loss? It wouldn't produce the same amount of pain. Only the actual losses you hope to cause—both political and financial—show the reader how the Boston Tea Party will hurt the British. Don't make the mistake of making the Resolution your plan to dump the tea. The plan here is merely a means to an end.

STEP 4: CATEGORIZE YOUR NOTES

The British have been provoking us for eight years, since the Stamp Act. Each time, we boycott and they repeal some or all of the taxes. But they always try again. **PROVOCATION**

We boycotted stamps, we boycotted the Townshend duties, and yet the tax on tea remains. **PROVOCATION**

Our battle cry, as you've often said, is "no taxation without representation" and this is an awful case of it. **PROVOCATION**

Lord North thinks he can trick us into accepting taxes on imports, like tea, but we won't accept it. **PROVOCATION**

We owe the British a big response after they killed five colonists in 1770. **PROVOCATION**

Philadelphia and New York turned the ships away, Charleston left the tea to rot in a warehouse, but here, Hutchinson insists the ships remain, and wants us to pay the duty. We must respond in a dramatic way. **PROVOCATION**

At Griffin's Wharf, three British ships sit. They're surrounded by armed ships of war. **PROVOCATION**

Commanders of the armed ships say that if we don't allow the tea to be unloaded by December 17, they will force it onto shore under cannon cover. **PROVOCATION**

These ships present an opportunity to force the Crown to recognize our rights as citizens. We lost much when Hutchinson allowed the ship to dock. If we don't act, the British will see Boston as a weak link in the resistance movement. **WHAT'S AT STAKE**

Hutchinson has also challenged us, by insisting he won't let the ships leave unless we pay the duty. He's trying to break us. **WHAT'S AT STAKE**

If we allow the East India Company to gain even a small foothold in Boston, they'll never let go. They need the money and won't hesi-

tate to use force once they see some of our people will buy their tea. **WHAT'S AT STAKE**

Therefore, we can't allow any of the tea to reach Boston. Loyalists will create a market for it and undercut the whole revolutionary movement. **WHAT'S AT STAKE**

I believe we ought to destroy the cargo. **PLAN**

We can dress as Mohawk Indians, disguise our faces with coal dust, and carry hatchets to use on the trunks of tea. **PLAN**

We can divide into three groups, each led by one man. One man should be assigned to approach the ship's captain and demand candles and the keys to the hold where the tea sits. **PLAN**

We should prepare some of our number to respond, in case the soldiers on the surrounding ships react. **PLAN**

We should use our hatchets to break open the chests and make sure the water can reach all the tea. **PLAN**

Once we've opened them all, dump them into the harbor. **PLAN**

The East India Company nearly bankrupted itself trying to expand trade into India. The loss of so much tea could ruin it. **BENEFITS**

Causing such a loss to the Company would be a direct slap to Lord North, who hopes to trick us into accepting taxation by selling us cheap tea. **BENEFITS**

It would also be a rebuke to Governor Hutchinson, who is not only a loyalist, but whose sons stand to gain from the tea sales as employees of the East India Company. **BENEFITS**

The East India Company announced plans to bring in its own agents to sell tea here in the colonies. This would hurt American merchants, cutting them out of the tea business altogether. **PROVOCATION**

STEP 5: CHOOSE DEVELOPMENT 3—POINT OF INSIGHT

The notes marked PLAN will show the reader that you really could cause the losses you mention in your Resolution. Your outline now looks this way:

You say:

Problem: We must cause
 the British pain so they'll
 stop taxing us.
Development 1 (Background):
Development 2 (Bridge):
Development 3 (Point of
 Insight): We should destroy
 the tea.
Resolution: Dumping the tea
 will hurt our enemies.

The reader says:
Yes, but how?

Yes!

Brilliant!

STEP 6: CHOOSE DEVELOPMENT 1—BACKGROUND

While Sam Adams knows about the Stamp and Townshend Acts, you can still use those pieces of information to help persuade him that this latest provocation requires a dramatic response. Therefore, the category PROVOCATION would make up your background Development. Your outline would now look this way:

You say:

Problem: We must cause
 the British pain so they'll
 stop taxing us.
Development 1 (Background):
 Provocation demands
 dramatic response.
Development 2 (Bridge):
Development 3 (Point of
 Insight): We should destroy
 the tea.

The reader says:
Yes, but how?

I can see your point.

Yes!

Resolution: Dumping the tea
will hurt our enemies.

Brilliant!

STEP 7: CHOOSE DEVELOPMENT 2—BRIDGE

The idea that connects the provocation we've endured and the response we plan to offer can be found in the category WHAT'S AT STAKE. In this case, the Bridge Development will increase the tension, so your reader nods his head more and more vigorously as he reads your argument. What's at stake? The enemy stands to lose money and face, but, if we take no action, we stand to lose, too. The revolutionary spirit could be crushed in Boston. All of this is in the notes and belongs in Development 2. Your outline is now complete:

You say:

Problem: We must cause
  the British pain so they'll
  stop taxing us.

Development 1 (Background):
  Provocation demands
  dramatic response.

Development 2 (Bridge):
  They stand to lose if we do
  this; we stand
  to lose if we don't.

Development 3 (Point of
  Insight): We should destroy
  the tea.

Resolution: Dumping the tea
  will hurt our enemies.

The reader says:
Yes, but how?

I can see your point.

The stakes are high!

Yes!

Brilliant!

STEP 8, PART 1: CREATE A LIST OUTLINE—ORGANIZE CATEGORIES AND DETAILS

The categories already placed are PROVOCATION, WHAT'S AT STAKE, and PLAN. But what about the BENEFITS category? That belongs in the Resolution, where we show the reader not just what our enemies stand to lose, but what they *would* lose if we succeed. What about the Problem chunk? In that, we need to simply orient Mr. Adams and present the Problem—We must cause the British pain so they'll stop taxing us.

This proposal addresses the tea problem we've been discussing. Given the situation, we have no choice but to respond to this latest provocation in a way that causes the British real pain, so they will stop taxing us once and for all.

Problem: We must cause the British pain so they'll stop taxing us.

PROVOCATION

Development 1 (Background): Provocation demands dramatic response.

WHAT'S AT STAKE

Development 2 (Bridge): They stand to lose if we do this; we stand to lose if we don't.

PLAN

Development 3 (Point of Insight): We should destroy the tea.

BENEFITS

Resolution: Dumping the tea will hurt our enemies.

STEP 8, PART 2: EVALUATE YOUR LIST OUTLINE

1. Do the notes within each chunk make the outline statement's point? **Yes. In general, the notes make the point of the outline statement they drive toward.**

2. Are the notes within each chunk organized logically? Do they move from one point to the next, gaining power with each new addition? **Some of the notes appear jumbled. In Development 1, the information on the colonists killed in 1770 interrupts notes about the tea crisis happening now. That information, since it refers to the fact that we owe the British a "big response" could be used as a transition into the end of the chunk, where we argue for such a response.**

3. Is the strongest point in each of the chunks at the end, nearest the outline statement? **In Developments 1 and 2, and in the Resolution, the weaker information often comes last. This must be rearranged for better effect. For example, in Development 1, the information that the East India Company plans to undercut local merchants isn't as compelling as the commander's threat to unload the tea under the cover of cannons.**

4. Is any important information missing? **Yes. Our Resolution could be made much stronger if we could quantify how much the East India Company actually stands to lose. How much tea do these boats carry? How much would be lost if we dumped them into the sea?**

STEP 8, PART 3: DO DIRECTED RESEARCH

The relevant facts can be found in Documents 2 and 3. The ships carried 342 chests of tea, with an estimated worth of 10,000 pounds sterling.

STEP 9, PART 1: ADD TRANSITIONS

1. A transition into Development 1 needs to move the reader back in time to the history of British provocation. Do that with a time transition, while introducing the idea of provocation that is the subject of this chunk: "For eight years, beginning with the Stamp Act and followed by the Townshend Duties, we've responded to British provocation with boycotts."

2. A transition into Development 2 might be as short and to the point as this: "We have too much at stake to fail." That drives directly into the point of the chunk—what we have at stake.

3. A transition into Development 3, our plan, could be equally quick: "My plan is the following:"

4. In the Resolution, you'll be summing up the benefits of your plan. Therefore, the transition into the chunk should be more complex. It should refer back to the previous section and remind the reader of the overall theme, which is that we want to cause the British real pain. Try something like this: "By taking quick and decisive action, we can damage our enemies and win a significant victory." The first phrase refers back to the plan, the rest speaks to the theme of the entire piece and the benefits we'll gain, which is the point the Resolution makes.

STEP 9, PART 2: WRITE AN OPENING HOOK

A proposal like this one requires a simple context narrative hook. Also, since it will likely be in letter form, don't forget to address it to Sam Adams. Your opening hook might look like this:

"Dear Sam,

Last night you requested I present a plan to respond to the problem of the unwelcome British tea shipment that sits in Boston Harbor."

This hook reminds Sam of your previous meeting and sets out immediately the subject of the proposal, which is a plan to deal with the unwanted tea shipment.

STEP 10: POLISH YOUR DRAFT

After you've turned notes into full sentences, polished and formatted your text, it should read something like this:

To: Sam Adams, Sons of Liberty

From: John Smythe

December 14, 1773

Dear Sam,

Last night you requested I present a plan to respond to the problem of the unwelcome British tea shipment that sits in Boston Harbor. It is my contention that this situation presents us with an unprecedented opportunity to advance our movement. If we can provide a painful consequence to the British in response to this latest provocation, we might deter them from taxing us again.

British Provocation

For eight years, beginning with the Stamp Act and followed by the Townshend Duties, we've responded to British provocation with boycotts. Though our refusal to buy goods resulted in repeal of some of the taxes, the British always return with new tax schemes designed to force our payments.

This latest duty is particularly offensive, as Lord North hopes to trick us into paying an import duty which is nothing more than another unfair tax on a staple of our diet. Now three East India Company ships sit at Griffin's Wharf. In a move intended to undercut colonial merchants, the Company has sent in its own agents holding exclusive contracts to sell tea to the colonies, thereby bypassing local distributors. To add insult to injury, the tea ships come flanked by warships, whose commanders plan to force us to accept their cargo under threat of cannon fire—all this while Governor Hutchinson insists the ships remain to force us to pay the duty.

In Philadelphia and New York, colonists succeeded in turning the ships back. In Charleston they accepted shipment, but left the tea to rot in the warehouses. Here in Boston we can do no less. Boycott is no longer enough; we must take dramatic action.

We have too much at stake to fail. If given a foothold in the colonies, the East India Company will likely resort to force to keep their markets open here. Also, loyalists in Boston will certainly create a market for British tea, undercutting the revolutionary movement.

We lost an opportunity when Hutchinson allowed the ships to dock. Now he's presented us with a clear challenge. We have no choice but to answer it. If we do, the advantages will be great, as we can strike a blow at the British, Hutchinson, and the East India Company at once.

Plan of Action

My plan is the following:

1. *On the night of the 16th, disguise 150 of our men as Mohawk Indians, faces darkened with coal dust.*

2. *Arm our men with tomahawks and split them into three groups, one for each ship.*

3. *Designate a group leader, several men to answer any fire from soldiers, and one man to approach the captain, to demand candles and directions to the tea.*

4. *Instruct the entire group to retrieve the tea, break open the trunks, and dump them into Boston Harbor.*

By taking quick and decisive action, we can damage our enemies and win a significant victory. The East India Company, nearly bankrupt after its India expansion, could be ruined by such an expensive loss. We will have sent a clear message to Lord North that pressing unwanted goods and taxes on the colonies will result in severe consequences. Finally, we'll have dealt with

Hutchinson, who thought to enrich his own sons, employees of East India, at our expense.

I hope you consider implementing the above plan without delay.

Sincerely,

John Smythe

Faithful Son of Liberty

INDEX